Musings from a Cluttered Mind

*A collection of short stories suitable
for the entire family*

By Rick Ryckeley

ThomasMax

Your Publisher
For The 21st Century

ACKNOWLEDGMENTS

First, I'd like to acknowledge Robert and Lee for their patience and tireless efforts holding my hand as this novice traverses the difficult path of printing. Thanks for the countless answered phone calls and emails; this is the first of many. Books - not phone calls or e-mails.

Second, a special thanks to Laura whom I often refer to as The English Teacher. Her knowledge and tolerance seem to have no limits even when I destroy the Queen's English and invent new words – both of which happen quite often. Thanks for making me look so good on paper.

Lastly, but really always first, I'd be remiss without thanking the one person who has been the source of most of my stories and all of my joy. Thanks, Becky, for putting up with me for so long.

Let me also say here that while every story within these pages is true, some names have been changed to protect the innocent…mainly me.

-- Rick Ryckeley
July 5, 2011

Musings from a Cluttered Mind

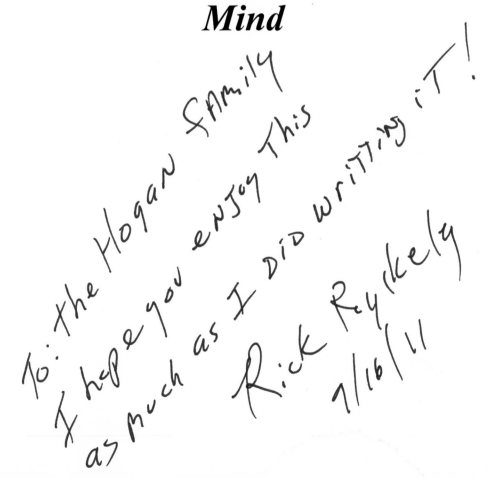

To: the Hogan family
I hope you enjoy this
as much as I did writting iT!
Rick Ryckely
7/16/11

ISBN-13: 978-0-9846347-2-9
ISBN-10: 0-9846347-2-X

First printing, August, 2011.

Cover design by Design Previews, Inc., DBA 11 Fingers

Published by:

ThomasMax Publishing
P.O. Box 250054
Atlanta, GA 30325
www.thomasmax.com

DEDICATION

This book is dedicated to not one, but two people. I know that's a little odd, but then again, so am I. The first dedication is to my loving and extremely understanding wife, Becky, who is named here in print for the first time. I was a firefighter many years before 9/11, and the incident affected me greatly - so much so that Becky suggested I write about it. The subsequent article found its way into our local newspaper - to the front page - and I've written a weekly column for that paper ever since. Becky, a school teacher at the time, didn't want her name in the paper so she suggested being called simply The Wife. So much more than "simply The Wife," she's my muse and the funniest, most intelligent person I've ever met. She is the joy in my life, the humor in my stories, and the loving wife of my dreams.

The second dedication goes out to my dad, who worked so tirelessly to support five children that he had little time left actually to spend with us. Through these stories, and the other six hundred not yet in book form, he has been able to enjoy and relive our childhoods that he missed out on. Thank you for your sacrifice, your continual guidance, and your love all these years. And thanks for not punishing me for all the things you now have found out about. Being a grounded 53-year-old would be hard to explain.

TABLE OF CONTENTS

Giving back – A portion of all book sales are donated to The *Go Two* Guys® Charitable Branch

The *Go Two* Guys charitable branch was established in 2010 by Rick and Becky Ryckeley. Our mission is to advance local injury and fire prevention efforts for those at greatest risk. We've given out car seats, bike helmets, batting helmets and safety equipment for local baseball teams. And in the future we'll donate money to help local fire department's fire safety education in elementary schools.

"Becky and I believed from the very start in giving back to the community. There were those who said, 'Why not wait until you make a profit before you donate?" Our answer was quick and simple, "Children are being hurt everyday by not having a car seat, bike or batting helmet. These are injuries that could've been prevented. The children, they don't have time to wait for us to make a profit. They need our help now. If not now, when? And if not us, who?"

The *Go Two* Guys®

Imagine one place where the residents of your community can go to find the help they need for any work done inside or outside their home – all done by someone they already trust: Their local off-duty firefighters!

The *Go Two* Guys® are local off-duty firefighters and experts in their field of service who serve the communities in which they live professionally and honorably. Each *Go Two* Guy brings that same devotion of service to your door.

As firefighters, we work a 24-hour shift and have 48 hours off. That's a lot of free time most people aren't afforded, and it gives us a unique opportunity to help others finally complete all of those "honey dos" around the house that they can't find the time for.

The *Go Two* Guys, Inc donates 2% of all income on a yearly basis to local injury and fire prevention efforts through our charitable branch. As our business grows, so will our commitment to the community. After all, we're firefighters. Giving back to the community is what we do.

In times of need, you turn to your family, and for over 400 years, firefighters have considered each other as family.

I look forward to **our** family helping **yours**.

Rick Ryckeley
The Go Two Guys' Head Guy
Visit our website for more details at www.TheGoTwoGuys.com

Observations of Life

Writing a weekly column since 2001, I have had many phone conversations with The English Teacher who corrects them, especially when it comes to my making up words – something I do quite often. It seems English teachers now and English teachers back in 1974 have something in common. They don't like it when they read words they've never seen before and can't pronounce. Welcome to my world. That's exactly the way I felt when trying to read Shakespeare for the first time.

It Done Got Complicated

Mrs. Newsome would have a duck fit over the title of this story. She was my tenth grade English teacher at Briarwood High School, home of the Mighty Buccaneers. After berating me once again about how I, single-handedly, hath destroyed the Queen's English, she would quickly follow up by asking, "And just how does a duck have a fit?"

For all you Neanderthals out there, I know my next statements go against the man code, but it's still true. I don't know everything, and I'll admit I've never figured out just how a duck can have a fit. Then again, it has become painfully apparent of late that there are a lot of things I don't know.

For example, this time last year I had a visit with my CPA. Tax season was once again looming on the horizon, and with all the new tax changes, an early trip to the number cruncher was prudent. Prudent – now Mrs. Newsome would've approved of my use of that word, and she would've really been impressed that it was used correctly in the sentence, but I digress.

For the last twenty-five years, I've been using the same number cruncher. And last year he said, "You need to start a business so you can have some write-offs. That way you won't pay so much in taxes next year." When the number cruncher speaks, I listen.

So in March of last year, The Wife and I borrowed a bunch of money and started a business. Unfortunately, we learned quickly that write-off for a business means you have to lose money – at least on paper. The business was to provide a service, to bring in extra money, to pay the taxes we owed, and show a loss (but not really lose money), so we don't have to pay taxes this year like we did last year. Like I said, it done got complicated.

Now that it's a year later, just how did we do? The business has done well, and with all the start-up costs, I thought we should have plenty of write-offs. With tax papers in hand and a bounce in my step, I happily walked into the number cruncher's office just knowing a big fat refund check was soon to be in our mailbox.

With papers piled high, we sat at one end of the long conference table. Ironically, I think the solid cherry table came from law firm that went out of business years ago. I guess they couldn't pay their taxes and had to sell everything.

For twenty minutes, I sat and anxiously watched as the number cruncher went line by line. Finally he sat back in his chair, removed his glasses, started to clean them, and said, "I've got some good news. You had some big losses due to start-up which are all deductible, but not all this year, and you had some income that threw you into a higher tax bracket."

I drew in a breath because I felt a "but" coming. I can always feel when there's a "but" coming. They're never good, and this time was no exception.

The number cruncher continued, "But the bottom line is I don't think you have to pay."

What! No big fat refund? On paper or not, I have to lose even more money to keep from paying taxes? Trying to figure out all this tax stuff…especially this year…well, it done got really complicated. I about had a duck fit right there on that ex-lawyer tax repossessed conference table! And I don't care what Mrs. Newsome has to say. If it looks like a duck fit, walks like a duck fit, then it's dad-gum duck fit.

Eight weeks before this book was submitted for publication, I did an interview with a local newspaper guy. Of all the questions the reporter could've asked, he asked, "There's no way with you being a firefighter that the Friday the 13th story could be true." My answer was simple, "Yes, the stories I tell are true. I can't make this stuff up – I'm not that good of a writer. The Wife's paper was for a student loan so she could continue her quest towards her Ph.D. She's the smart one in our family, but most of my readers already know that. Her two hours of work were wiped out due to the electrical outage I had caused. And finally – yes, firefighters do stupid things like everyone else. Most just don't write about it in the newspaper."

Friday 13th

Yesterday, looking down from the top of my ladder, I saw a black cat with big yellow eyes lying underneath and staring back up at me. Right then, I should have known things were going to go awry. Moments later, everything went dark. The Wife heard a loud THUD and ran upstairs. It was me falling off the ladder after shocking myself and shorting out the lights.

She entered the room and looked down with concern etched in her face; the eight-foot step ladder I had been climbing lay next to me. Our black cat with big yellow eyes sat atop my chest and meowed. She was looking down at me too, although I didn't notice concern etched in her face – too much fur. This was just the start of my attempt to install a ceiling fan. After eight hours involving two trips to the doctor's office, one ace bandage, one icepack, and one stern lecture about the dangers of electricity, the ceiling fan was finally installed, but that's how the story ends. Here's how it starts.

Sporting giant oak leaf blades and a large, frosted globe light, the new fan we bought at the giant hardware store with the orange roof would lend the perfect ambiance for the writing studio, a.k.a. the bonus room over the garage. Installing it should've been a simple enough task. Besides how hard could it be? If I got into trouble, I could simply read the instructions.

Ms. Newsome, my tenth grade English teacher, said that the English language can be a very useful tool – especially if you're one of those people who actually read instructions. And if you are a regular reader of this column, you already know I'm not one of those people.

Arriving back home, I lugged the heavy box upstairs, opened it, and pulled out all the pieces. There was so much stuff that it looked like someone had dumped all the parts from three fans into one box. Then I did what any real man would never do. Looked around to make sure The Wife was nowhere near, opened the instructions, and tried to read them.

The instructions were a twenty-page book printed in five different languages with excellent illustrations that really would've helped – if one of the five different languages had actually been English. Frustrated, I threw the instructions in the corner. Yellow eyes immediately thought this was an invitation to play "shred the instruction booklet into a thousand little pieces."

With all hope for any kind of instructional help lost, I removed the old light fixture. I know you're supposed to cut off the electricity first, but I did cut off the light switch. This, I found out too late, wasn't the same as cutting off the electricity.

To make sure the heavy fan wouldn't fall, I used two four-inch screws to secure the bracket holding the fan to the ceiling. The screws went through the ceiling, through the wood 2 x 4 in the attic, and through the wire going to the switch – which was still energized. That's how I shorted out the lights, fell off the ladder, and landed with a THUD on the floor.

I don't know if The Wife wanted to make sure the black cat didn't get hurt or me. But the rest of the day she stayed in the bonus room under the guise of working on the computer. For the next two hours, we both worked on our tasks. I was installing the ceiling fan; The Wife was working on student loan forms, ready to call 911 for help if I fell again. Finally, I proudly walked over to the light switch and announced, "The fan is now installed."

In the twelve years of our marriage, some things I've done haven't been too smart. Cutting on that light switch falls into the "not too smart" category. In an instant, the breaker in the basement tripped and all the power to the bonus room cut off – along with all the unsaved government forms The Wife had been working on for the last two hours. Yellow Eyes wisely exited the room.

The Wife said, "Please call Mitch for help before you burn down our house." I'm sure she was mad; I just couldn't see her because the lights were out. I started down the steps to make the call, tripped on Yellow Eyes that was lying in wait for me on the landing, fell the rest of the way, and landed in a crumpled mass at the bottom. The cat then jumped on my chest and started to purr.

After we got back from the doctor the second time, I called Best Friend Mitch. He told me how to fix the fan. Unfortunately he couldn't do anything about the government forms being wiped out by the electrical shortage or The Wife being mad. Today is Friday the 13th, and my black cat is still staring at me with those big yellow eyes. No telling what'll happen.

There's a small lake in the middle of a park just down from our house. Whenever I need time to think and relax, I walk down to the park. The day this story was written was just such a time. Trying to write a story about how and why one group of people moves away from another is hard to do without offending someone. Thankfully, the inhabitants of the lake and the little white duck were the perfect metaphors to illustrate such a flight.

Little White Duck

A lone little white duck floated on the waters. Small ripples followed close behind as he paddled around the only place he had known as home. The surroundings were familiar to him, and in that familiarity he drew solace. He was aware of his differences from all the other inhabitants and knew his status. Even so, he was happy and satisfied just being a duck – a duck that lived on a lake – a lake that teemed with a great diversity of other life. But he was still lonely being the only duck.

On the southern end of the lake lived a family of mud turtles sunning themselves on fallen logs – ready to slip beneath the surface and into the safety of the muddy shoreline at the first hint of danger. They ignored the little white duck as he neared. It was an easy thing to do. After all, he was different and didn't look like any turtle they had ever seen before. Residents of the lake for much longer than he, they didn't consider him a threat and nor really worth their time away from the important job of sunning.

With a quack hello, the duck paddled past and over to a pair of loons. One white, the other gray – they stood on spindly legs in the shallow waters of the stream inlet waiting for the morning sun and breakfast. Reeds, indiscernible from the loons' spindly legs, choked the inlet and provided not only the ideal cover for the loons, but a smorgasbord of bugs. They bobbed their heads slightly in acknowledgment and then ignored the little white duck as they snapped up the water bugs. After all, he wasn't one of their kind. Once again he gave a friendly quack and paddled past.

Mid-day, a flock of Canadian geese skimmed the surface of the lake and then landed with a splash. Ripples rocked the little white duck but didn't deter him. He paddled over to investigate the newest visitors to his watery home. He remembered they had come about this time last year and had ignored him. Maybe this year it would be different. The geese were brown with black necks and twice his size. One or two were even white just like him. Still small by their standards, he was much larger than a year ago. Surely they'd welcome him to their flock – especially the ones that looked like him. After all, birds of a feather do flock together, don't they? They didn't. Instead, they spent the afternoon diving underwater for food, all the while swimming away from him.

Apart from all others, two snow white swans sat on the banks of the northern shore. Their long graceful necks intertwined in a loving embrace as they groomed each other. Such graceful and beautiful creatures, surely they wouldn't mind if he spent some time with them. Waddling up on shore, he quacked his friendliest hello. Their reaction wasn't what he expected. In an instant the once beautiful creatures turn ugly. Flapping their wings, they pecked and squawked at the duck, driving him back into the water – away from their sunny spot.

Rejected once again, the lonely little duck paddled away. He finally understood. Even though all life on the lake had similarities, all were indeed different. And some of those differences could never be overcome, especially if only one party is willing and the other is not. For the rest of the afternoon, the inhabitants kept to their part of the lake – seldom visiting one another. When the turtles crawled up on a new log too close to the loons, the loons moved. As the Canadian geese paddled over to visit, the graceful swans flew to another part of the lake. The swans isolated themselves from all others, believing themselves to be better than the rest.

A great sadness came over me at the end of the day as I watched the little white duck circle the lake in search of someone who was similar. Finally, The Wife and I called him over. He waddled up on shore, gobbling bread and our leftover french-fries. For a moment he seemed happy. Someone, though very different than he, had cared enough to pay attention to his needs – and in return had received great joy from doing so.

Like the inhabitants of the lake, all of us are different, but we're all the same. And moving away from one part of the lake to another just because of status is not the answer to getting along. It's the problem. Ignorance fosters contempt. This year, visit a shelter and lend a helping hand or read a book at a retirement home. And when you're done, visit your new neighbors and get to know them and their differences. After all, it's our differences that make us all stronger.

Men are just big babies, and I'm not too proud to admit it. Dad used to say, "If the shoe fits, then get them out of the floor – they're yours." The Wife reminded me of this nugget of wisdom when she tripped over my shoes in the middle of the floor and asked whom they belonged to. I love The Wife, and I'm sure glad she loves babies.

Men Are Just Babies

This is another article that could get me kicked out of the men's club, but someone has to write about it, and it might as well be me. Old sayings tend to be sprinkled with a lot of truth – old sayings like "He married someone that reminded him of his mother." Let's face it, guys, when it comes right down to it – we're all just a bunch of babies. Man Babies.

See, I told you this article would get me in a lot of hot water with my fellow Neanderthals out there. But I'm sorry, men are just big babies who want to be pampered and coddled throughout life. I know. I'm one of them. And I'm not too proud to admit it. When The Wife does those little extra things to make my life more comfortable, I like it. Yes, I'm a man baby.

Being a man baby is not so bad. It has many advantages – much like being a little baby. They're very similar. You disagree? Well, maybe I can convince you otherwise with a comparison of the small baby you hold in your arms and the big baby your wife holds in hers – the big baby being you, of course.

When little babies are hungry, they cry, and if you don't feed them quickly, they cry even louder and get really grumpy. When they get their bottle and they're fed, everything's fine. The Wife says that when I skip lunch, I get really, really grumpy at about five in the afternoon and I'm hard to be around. The only way I stop being grumpy is when she fixes me a little snack to tide me over until dinner.

Still don't see the comparison? Here's another example: babies can't do anything for themselves – like laundry. If you didn't pick up after a baby, there would be laundry strewn all over the house: baby bibs, blankets, itsy-bitsy socks, night clothes. Little babies create an inordinate amount of dirty laundry. Man babies do too, and I speak from years of experience on this topic. I can go through three to four different sets of clothes in just one day – workout clothes in the morning, tee shirt and blue jeans during the day, sweats to lounge around in after dinner, and PJ's at bedtime. Most of these never make the trip to laundry room. Still haven't convinced you that men are just big babies? Well, read on, dear reader, read on.

One of the best things little babies do is they make all those strange noises and facial gestures. They gurgle, giggle, and coo – all the while entertaining us with the expressions on their faces. Men babies are no different – they make funny faces and sounds too. When I get up after sitting too long in front of the computer or the day after that long golf game, I make a face distorted with pain. Old muscles resent being used. The noises from my creaking joints are heard down the hallway as I make my way to the hot tub for some relief.

Here's one last comparison between little babies to the man babies out there. Little babies will scream and throw a temper tantrum until they get what they want. Man babies do the same thing. Ever wanted to buy something and your wife said no? What did you do? I tell you what you did; you bugged her and pouted till you got it, right? I rest my case, Man Baby.

There's another old saying that kinda goes like this: If the wife ain't happy, ain't nobody happy – not even the man baby around the house. And she ain't gonna be happy if she has to do all the cooking, laundry, and cleaning the house all by herself. Especially if, after working all day taking care of the kids or working outside the home, she comes back at dinner time and has to then take care of her big Man Baby. Like I said, there's a lot of truth in those old sayings.

So all you man babies out there, get up off the couch; your favorite baseball team can win without you tonight. Get your own adult beverage – you can drink it while you cook dinner. And while you're at it, the laundry monster is getting out of hand. It's not gonna kill you to help out just a little around the house. See, I told you; a lot of hate e-mail will be coming my way because of this one, but this man baby's too busy to read any of it right now. It's time to cook dinner, and there's a huge load of laundry that needs to be folded. The Wife will be home soon.

This story wrote itself after I had spent a long day and longer night working at the fire department. On the way home, I got behind a slow driver. At the grocery store, I got in the shortest line. Unfortunately the person in front of me had coupons that were out of date, forgot something down aisle two, and wanted to argue about sale items. The teenagers in the parking lot cut off an elderly couple almost knocking them down as they ran to their cars. Patience for me is truly a lifelong pursuit.

Patience Is a Lifelong Quest

Having passed the half-century mark, it is safe to say that there are a few things I've picked up along the way. For example: when the dog barks at night, he ain't just saying hello. He needs to be walked. That's why he's barking. If you still have teenagers and you want to get a good night's sleep, lock the bedroom door, take the phone off the hook, and simply ignore any and all noise outside the bedroom. And when The Wife says, "Don't get too tired today, Honey," she has an ulterior motive. Believe me, if you get too tired, you'll never find out what it is.

Over the years the things I've learned could fill volumes. And in all that information there is one item that has eluded me – patience. It has been said patience is a virtue. Guess it's one I will never possess. No matter how old I am, there're some things in this world that I have little patience for.

I understand young folks today want to listen to "their" music. And it's their right. I'm sure my parents thought the music I listened to was just as bad and radical as I find The Boy's, although I don't remember the Beatles singing about killing cops or beating women. Their music was about peace and love. Yep, I can see how those radical Beatles had a terrible influence on me and society. Funny, their "mind numbing" music has lasted for over forty years. I doubt the kids of today are going to be humming the tunes of any rap artist a year from now much less forty. Rap music – now there's something I have zero patience for.

Regardless of what music you're listening to if, at a red light, it shakes parts of my car loose, I quickly run out of all patience. In other words, your music rights end at my ear. Patience is a lifelong quest. In the area of music appreciation and tolerance for loud decibels, it's one I'm proud to say I won't live long enough to achieve.

When we were young, Dad use to say, "You kids have to respect your elders. You'll want people to respect you when you get old." Now that I'm older, I want that respect. And I have little if any patience when I don't receive it. Sorry, when someone older than you or your parents asks you a question, a grunt isn't an appropriate response. It's a grunt. That's what pigs do. Then again, after a quick look into most teenagers' bedrooms, maybe a grunt is an appropriate response after all.

I have little patience when it comes with postponing the "I wants." I just don't like to wait. I want to go on an expensive vacation now, not when we really can afford it. I want that new Smart car. It doesn't matter that I can't fit into it. The newer larger models won't be out until next year, and I don't want to wait. My lack of fortitude for the "I wants" extend to the bills when they come due. I want not to pay them.

Lastly, as sweet as she is, sometimes I don't even have patience when it comes to The Wife. I don't want to wait until this evening to see her. I think I'll surprise her with a picnic lunch. I wonder if I could convince her boss to let her have the rest of the day off. I'm sure he'll understand. The pile of work on her desk will not get finished, phone calls and e-mails won't get returned, but she'll get it all done first thing in the morning. All he has to do is have a little patience.

People ask me how I've come up with material to write over 600 short stories – Where do I get all the ideas? It's really simple: all I do is look around, listen, and then write. Just like the story below.

Every Window a Stage

It could've been entitled *A Snapshot of Small Town America: A Short Film Suitable for All Ages*. Admission was free – free for all who had taken the time to sit, sip, and simply watch the show. Sipping a vanilla chai and enjoying the ambiance the small town coffee shop had to offer, I sat and pondered how seemingly simple yet complex the world outside the picture window was. Having nothing better to do, I decided to watch for a while.

First on the world stage outside the window, a middle-aged lady wearing a skin-tight shirt sauntered by singing, "Bringing Sexy Back."

She wasn't.

Next appearing outside the window was Supermom! Who else could she be? While balancing a baby on one hip and an armload of Black Friday deals on the other, she was followed by two young children who were playing the proverbial childhood game of "Don't Touch Me" as she walked serenely to her car with a smile on her face. Any mom who can do that and not scream at the children trailing farther and farther behind is certainly a Supermom in my book. Either that or she was smiling because the children trailing behind weren't hers.

I shifted my weight on the stool, took another sip of my chai, and continued to enjoy the sideshow unfolding on the stage on the other side of the window.

Parked next to the old furniture building across the street was Officer Tom – a veteran member of the police force. He, too, was waiting patiently, sitting in his cruiser, sipping coffee, and watching the show but through a very different window – a window tinted with the stresses of his job and the duty to protect and serve the citizens of this small town.

As if on cue, the newest stop sign in town was once again ignored as a light blue sedan rushed through the intersection in front of him. Officer Tom stopped his sipping and sprang into action, his cruiser's blue lights bouncing off the crumbling stucco wall of the old furniture building as he pulled away from the curb. It was his time to enter the show and start acting. Good cop, bad cop? It was totally up to the occupant of the light blue sedan. I've known Tom for years. He would give the occupant of the sedan a break if he could.

The waitress brought me a complimentary muffin. Being a regular does have its perks. The coffee shop owners recently hired a new chef, and I was in the right place at the right time to sample her latest creation – the Blueberry Monster. I sat, sipped, and munched as the next cast member entered from stage right. It was the city manager.

Into the view of my window ambled Steve, skillfully performing the balancing act of his office once again. City manager for the last ten years, he was known by residents as an honest family man who worked tirelessly at his job. He cheerfully greeted and shook hands with all who passed. The short walk down from City Hall was always a welcome afternoon break. As of late, though, the stresses of reduced revenues, increased expenses, and afternoons filled with budget meetings caused him to change his mid-afternoon routine to mid-morning. Still, for the time it took him to drink a cup of coffee, he sat, sipped, and greeted the people – then exited the show stage left.

Finally finished with my chai and having defeated the Blueberry Monster, it was time for me to enter the show from backstage and lend a helping hand on set. The light blue sedan had returned, and it seemed that Officer Tom had only given the driver a warning after all. The sedan was full of excited children who helped Dad select and cut down their tree. The prized Christmas tree had been loosely tied to the top of the sedan and had just toppled off the roof of the car as it rounded the corner in front of my window. I left my perch and helped the frazzled father secure the tree to the top with the carload of tots as a joyful audience.

Cars, stores, or home, there are windows everywhere. This holiday season take the time to sit, sip, and watch the show outside with your loved ones, and when the time arrives, lend a helping hand to a frazzled neighbor. Kindness has a ripple effect, and there's no way to tell how many lives those ripples might touch. And who knows, there may even be a Blueberry Monster in your future.

I spent six months in the strange world of the Left-Handers, and the time I spent there proves the old saying "You don't really know someone until you walk a mile in their shoes." Luckily, my time spent in the left-handed world was brief. There're some that have to spend their entire lives there. How they function day to day, I'll never know.

Stuck in the World of Left-Handers

Congratulations! If you're reading this, it looks like you made it into the New Year, and since I'm writing it, it looks like I've made it as well. As I look back at the holiday, I think things could've gone a bit better. Having both major shoulder surgery five days before Christmas and everyone over at our house for a family reunion might not have been the greatest idea after all.

Although the shoulder operation was really bad timing, it did accomplish the goal of saving my life. The Wife said if I didn't stop complaining about the pain and just go ahead and get fixed…well, you can finish her sentence. Unfortunately, my right shoulder was the one that got fixed and I'm right-handed. So until the doctor says otherwise, I'm stuck in the strange world of left-handers.

After five days of exploring this new world, I thought there was no way anyone could do anything using just their left hand. Now, at the end of the first week, I'm sure of it. Being left-handed is really difficult. I'm having such a hard time adjusting that I think I'm going to apply for a handicap sticker for my car.

After ten days, I had a follow-up with the doctor. He informed me not to bother with the handicap permit. It seems I'll be in a sling for two more months and won't be able to drive anyway. Great, I guess that's just something else added to the list of things I can't do. Just what else is on the impossible list for the newbie left-hander? Just read on, dear reader, read on.

At the top of my list is typing on a computer keyboard using just the fingers of the left hand. Even though they appear to be the same appendages as the ones on the right hand, they seem to have a mind of their own. Sure, there are computer programs out there that'll write what you say, but I've found they all seem to have the same design flaw. They understand many languages, but none understand Southern. Take it from me, this hunt and peck stuff is really slow. I can't even type 100 words a minute – not that I could before my operation, but the doctor did say he'd make me better so I was really hoping that meant I would be able to type faster.

Next on the list of impossible things to do left-handed is tying one's own shoes. And yes, I could do that before I hurt my shoulder. Lucky for me, The Wife now does that for me as soon as I pull them on. I guess she doesn't want me to trip over any untied shoelaces and break something else.

Wrapping presents and using scissors are two more impossible tasks. A left-hander using right-handed scissors just doesn't work. NOTE TO SELF – buy left-handed scissors. Also buy left-handed can opener, television remote, self-opening adult beverage bottles, a left-handed razor, pen and a self-peeling banana. Oh, most important of all, buy left-handed toilet paper.

It's been two weeks now since the surgery, and The Wife's back at work. I don't think I'm going to make it in this left-handed world all alone. I need to find a support group like Left-Handers Anonymous. And to think, there's people out there that actually have been left-handers all of their lives! How they function day to day with such a handicap is a mystery to me. I'd shake their hand, but I don't have the left-handed hand shake down yet.

I guess left-handers are indeed better than right-handers. Not only can they survive in the right-handed world, but they can function with ease in the strange and difficult world of left-handers. Right now, stuck in their world, I'd be happy just to be able to tie my shoes.

The little boy and his dad never knew how they affected me. They never knew this story was written. I was spending too much time in the past and not enough time in the present. For me, from this moment on, our yearly family reunions took on an entirely different light.

Two Little Green Froot Loops

It was early in the morning when it happened. A little boy and his dad had just left the lobby of the hotel with their complimentary breakfasts. In his hands the dad held two coffees, muffins, a plate of fresh fruit, and milk for his son's cereal. Obviously, Mom was sleeping in. The little boy, about three years old, carried very carefully a bowl of Froot Loops. As they rounded the corner to the elevator, the little boy bumped into the wall – spilling two green Froot Loops onto the floor. He looked down at them as they rolled around and came to rest at his bare feet. When they did, he looked up at his dad and said, "Uh-oh."

His dad answered, "Don't worry son; you still have a whole bowl full." Both kept walking to the elevator, where his dad stopped to push the button. The little boy, still looking back – worrying about the two little green Froot Loops he had dropped and left behind – bumped into his dad and spilled the entire bowl onto the floor.

I met some people at our family reunion last month – people I hadn't seen since I was a little boy myself. Though their outward appearance had changed somewhat, they were the same on the inside – the same as I remembered them so many years ago.

The Sister was at the reunion, the same sister that got mad when we pulled her hair and ran to Mom when we hid her Barbie dolls. She's now a marine biologist. She told me about the 500 acres of trees that she will plant this year, turning farm land into a new forest and wildlife habitat. A correct mixture of trees must be planted in order to bring in wildlife, and that's her job. An all-pine forest would mean a forest barren of life.

The Sister gave us a gift of two walking sticks with semi-precious gems set into them. The sticks she made, and both were twisted by vines from top to bottom. The Sister told us that one walking stick was smooth because it didn't resist the vine as it grew. The other walking stick was knotted and rough because it resisted and had a hard time growing. Looking back over my youth, I feel like that second walking stick.

Big Brother James was at the reunion, the big brother that showed me how to shave the first time with short, quick, jerky motions. He was the brother who was a terror on the high school football field for five years and a three-time state wrestling champion. He was there with his wife, 13-year-old daughter and a new baby girl.

James talked about his plans for a new land development with sidewalks, nature trails, and elevated cart paths. It will keep him busy for many years to come – so will that teenage daughter. The land development is truly visionary and beautiful, but not nearly as much as his new baby girl.

Twin Brother Mark was also at the reunion, the twin brother with whom I shared a bedroom and many a Batman comic book for the first fifteen years of life. The brother I seemed to always be in a fight with, the brother who always got picked last at the games we played. But in the game of life, it seems that Mark has finished first. Last April, he retired after twenty years of serving his country as an Air Force pilot. With a wife, an eight-year-old son, and a one-year-old baby boy, he also retired a very rich man.

Older Brother Richard and Mom couldn't make the family reunion this year. They were having a reunion of their own. They both were in another place, waiting on all of us to join them. Looking around at the family, I could see a part of them in all of our faces.

The little boy was so busy looking back at what he had lost he didn't see that what he held in his hands was so much more. Like that little boy, I've concentrated on looking back at something that I too have lost: my childhood and the time growing up with my brothers and sister, so much so I haven't seen what I'm holding in my hands: the time I now can spend with them and their families as grown adults.

Okay, I'll admit it: I'm a workaholic. Admitting you have a problem is the first step to recovery. I tried so hard to relax on our vacation that it stressed me out so much I had to go back to work just to rest. So I wrote this story while The Wife took a nap. Please don't tell her it was during our vacation.

Vacation Rules

After four days in the North Carolina mountains with The Wife, I came back rested, relaxed, and with an updated list of vacation rules. Yes, dear reader, even vacations have rules. And if you want an enjoyable relaxing time with your better half, print these out and follow them to the letter. You'll thank me later.

To start, this is not a complete list of rules. To print all of them would take too much space so I've listed the most important ones. Those would be the ones that came up during last week's trip. What is at the top of the list? Don't, for any reason, disturb The Wife during nap time. And while on vacation, naptime can occur at any time.

Almost as important as the first rule is the second. When you go on vacation, diets also go on vacation. If you suggest otherwise, you will be not rested and relaxed, but battered and bruised upon your return.

The next one is the hard one. You must magically forget about all those things that worry you during your daily life while you're on vacation. You know – all that stuff that caused you to need a vacation in the first place. The shrinking value of your home, mounting bills, and all those problems at work must not be talked about endlessly. All must be forgotten, not mentioned whatsoever, and above all else, not worried about while on vacation! Sorry, my love, I'll work on this one.

If you have kids this next rule is for you. Never, ever, bring the kids on the grownup vacation. If you want to, you can go on their vacation each year, but each year you and your better half must take your own vacation without them. What? You mean you actually brought kids with you? Well, let me introduce you to rule number four.

Never bring kids on a grownup vacation, especially if the kids you bring aren't your own. If your son or daughter wants to bring their friend on vacation, this is what you should say, "When you're grown, moved out with a job of your own, then and only then can you bring your best friend with you on vacation. By then, they won't be your best friend, but if you still want them to go, it's fine. Besides you'll be paying for everything at that time not us."

Saying anything else will certainly lead to disaster, and it will not be a relaxing time for you or the wife. And if it's Spring Break in Panama City Beach, Florida, the only ones guaranteed to have a good time are the kids. You'll just have to trust me on this one. A five-hour drive, 72 hours without sleep, multiple unanswered cell phone calls, and I didn't even get a T-shirt.

Now that the kids have been left at home, the next rule comes into play. Don't, for any reason, call home to check on them, the pets, or plants. Don't laugh; I know this guy who's really fond of his giant cactus. And no, it's not me. Mine died two years ago. I really miss Sticky.

The second part of rule number six is even harder to obey. Don't take any phone calls from the kids. If you thought they were old enough to be left at home alone in the first place, they should be old enough to handle any emergency that comes up in your absence. Besides, they just have to remember how to dial 911; that's three numbers. And if it's really bad, that's why you have insurance.

Whether it's a day get-a-way, a romantic weekend in the mountains, or even that rare five day/four night vacation you always cut short by one day – make sure to remember the most important rule of all. The time spent with the one you love is time you will never get again.

A former firefighter and best friend for twenty-five years, Mitch has always been there for me. When his mom passed, like a good friend, I was there for him. We don't get to choose how we come into this world or how we go out – only how we live. We don't talk to children about death or how fleeting life really is, but maybe we should. That way they would value life even more.

Everything we say or do can have an effect on someone we leave behind. Whether it's positive or negative is completely up to you.

When I Was Small

When I was small my best friend suddenly stopped coming around to play. Mom said, "He's moved on to a better place." Being five and all, I thought that meant his family had moved to the Duke of Gloucester. That's where all the rich people lived. And if you asked any of them, it was a much better place than Flamingo Street. I was wrong.

His family did leave Flamingo Street, but it wasn't because they wanted to live on the Duke. They left because the memories of their only child filled the house. It was a loss too great for his parents to bear. When all else is gone, for better or worse, memories of ones that have moved on still remain. They bring warmth to some hearts because of what was, and break other hearts because of what might have been.

When I was a little older, Sam dropped out of Old Mrs. Crabtree's third grade class. Sam was the richest kid at Mt. Olive Elementary. We all thought he was on another vacation to some distant and exciting land. We were wrong. Mrs. Crabtree told us that Sam had "passed on" and was in a better place. Bully Brad blurted out, "How do you know he's in a better place? He's dead." Brad's screams echoed down the hallway as Mrs. Crabtree dragged him to the office by his ear.

Strange, it was the very same question I was going to ask. I guessed it comforted Sam's parents to believe he was indeed in a better place. Besides, at the time, I really didn't know where Sam was or where he ended up. Who was I to argue about such things? I was just a kid in the third grade.

When I was at Auburn University, everyone was so full of life. We all thought we were invincible. Although Death often visited the campus, students rarely spoke about it. If one of us had proven they were not invincible, that meant the rest of us weren't either. That was a concept our young minds could not fully comprehend.

When asked, our professors explained the act of dying simply as transitioning to another plane of existence. This we could accept. After all, another plane of existence, wherever it was, was still an existence. It wasn't death. Besides who was I to argue. I was just a college kid.

Now that I'm over fifty, I guess I look at death differently than most. At the end of life, it's like being in a small room – one door has to close before another one opens. Only then can we walk through to the other side. This week, Best Friend Mitch lost a loved one. She has walked through that final door. This will be his first Thanksgiving without his mother. Our prayers and thoughts are with him, his father, and their family. The day will certainly be different, but he still has his memories of his time with her, and as long as we keep the memories of the people we love alive, they will indeed live forever.

On Thanksgiving, call or visit the ones you love. Mend any broken fences and simply enjoy being alive. Our time together is short. Hug the kids and grandchildren and eat good home cooking. Savor the life that you have. What I know now, I didn't know when I was five, couldn't understand when I was in third grade, and didn't want to believe when I was in college. No matter how much we don't want it to, one day our life will also transition and memories will be all our loved ones have of us. This holiday make memories with your family and friends that will last them forever.

College was the only thing in my life that I ever quit. It was a decision that framed the next thirty years in ways, both good and bad, that I never could imagine. Finally, at age 51, I received my diploma and wrote this story. Funny, only one person looks at me differently now than before – and that's me. I guess that's all that matters. The voices are finally silenced.

Something Quite Extraordinary

There are times in a person's life that are truly defining points. Times that will be remembered forever – a first kiss, marriage, and the birth of a child. One such defining moment happened last weekend, and it was quite extraordinary. It wasn't the fact that I turned 51 on Saturday – although it is a truly amazing thing to think about. I've been on this spinning blue globe for over half a century – fewer days now lie ahead than behind me.

Still, it seems like just yesterday I was playing with the guys back on Flamingo Street and running for my life whenever Bully Brad came lurking around. Thinking about it though, I guess one doesn't really have to do anything to get older – other than not die. But not many consider that feat to be extraordinary. Unless, of course, growing up they had Bully Brad as a next-door neighbor.

It's true that the extraordinary thing that occurred last Saturday meant more to me than it did to anyone else. I righted the biggest mistake of my life with a simple push of a button. The huge weight that I've been carrying around for thirty years finally fell away. Alone at the time, except for the gray and black cat asleep on my lap, there was no fanfare and it wasn't covered by any television broadcast. Newspapers around the area didn't run any headlines – although they probably should have. The first person I called was The Wife. "I've submitted my last paper. You're now talking to a college graduate."

College is the only thing in my life I ever quit. What now seems a lifetime ago, I left Auburn University after three years of study without a degree in order to start down a different path than my brothers and sister – all of whom graduated. At first, it was spoken of many times at family reunions. Rightly or not, I felt like less of a person because I was the only one who didn't finish. Eventually, like many family secrets, it was swept into a closet only to reappear when least expected, bringing with it the same pain and shameful regret. "He's the only one that didn't finish."

It would be a lie to say with each birthday it got easier to look back at that mistake and accept it. The farther I got away from it, the heavier the burden seemed to become. Will doors that have been closed to me now magically open because I have a degree? We'll see. What I do know is that those mocking voices in my head from long ago have finally been silenced, and I feel better about myself. That's what really matters.

If you have anything in your life that you've left undone, anything that you've quit, or anything you always wanted to do, you owe it to yourself to do it. Don't wait thirty years like I did. Create a defining point in your life now. Remember the only person that can complete you is you. And if you don't do it, this spinning blue globe will surely be incomplete, whether you have a college degree or not.

I've finally learned you don't have to know how to do everything. You just have to know who to call. And when it comes to anything about computers, The Boy is the one to call. But don't. If he's helping you, then he won't have time to help me.

You Must Have Protection

The following is going to make me sound like an out-of-touch old guy, but I'm fine with that. This story happened just as written, and for once, there has been no embellishment by yours truly. One thing that just really gets my goat (now that's an old guy term if I ever heard one) is buying something and having it not work once you get it home. Case in point – the $100 anti-virus computer program I bought last weekend.

For those non-computer people out there, it seems that computers can get viruses. They can also be infected by worms, Trojans, and spies. Although if you don't go onto the internet, it seems your computer will never come down with any of these afflictions. You'll never be able to connect with anyone, but that's beside the point. At least it will be safe from all those nasty beasties.

If you do want to venture out into cyberspace, then you must have protection – hence the reason for my purchase of the latest virus protection software. Once home, all I had to do was stick the disk into my computer, the program would run, and all would be fine – protected once again. Fortunately, that didn't happen. I say fortunately because if it had, I would have had to find something else to write about this week.

When the program didn't work, I called my son, The Boy, for help. After twenty frustrating minutes on the phone, the program still didn't work so he said, "Just call the company." A nice machine at the company put me on hold and advised me every few minutes not to hang up or I would lose my place in line. With the phone on speaker, I started to do push-ups and sit-ups – might as well get in a quick workout while waiting.

Over a half hour later, the nice machine still advised me not to hang up. By this time, I had completed over 100 push-ups and 130 sit-ups. Getting tired, I decided to try another tactic. Reading the box the program came in, I found the company's website. With no protection, I still took a chance and entered a place I had never been before – a chat room. Cassandra was waiting to assist me.

For you non-computer people out there, a chat room works just like a telephone – except there's no phone. You carry on a conversation by typing questions to someone like Cassandra. A few quick questions and answers were typed, and she said she could fix my problem, but first she asked permission to take control of my computer. I thought it was a joke because she was in India so I told her she could. It seems the joke was on me.

My computer cut itself off, then back on, programs opened and then closed. Somehow Cassandra had taken complete control all the way from across the world! In less than ten minutes, she fixed the program and I had all the protection I needed to surf the web. I thanked her, and she left the chat room. I suddenly felt lonely so I cut the lights off and left the room too. Don't want to waste any electricity, now do we?

When The Wife got home, I told her about how someone from India took control of my computer and did amazing things. She smiled and said, "You know Cassandra really didn't have to ask permission, she could've taken control anytime she wanted. You weren't protected."

Now that's a scary thought. The next time my computer gets a virus, and I'm no longer protected, I have the perfect solution – one that doesn't involve doing push-ups, sit-ups, or calling Cassandra. A way to truly protect all the sensitive information stored. No one will ever be able to hack my computer if I just throw it out the second story window onto the driveway. Problem solved, and I didn't even have to call The Boy.

As a writer, I keep a small notebook with me at all times – in my pocket, in the car, and next to the bed. I look, listen, and then write down a word or phrase that can be used in a story at a later date. Just before drifting off to sleep or right after waking up I have my best ideas for stories. Like this one.

Dreamland

Early in the morning is usually when it happens. Before the first yellow-orange finger rays of sunlight reach across the sky and screen their way through the blinds, there is but a moment. A special moment in time when dreams and reality mix before the fine line between them slowly ebbs away in the cool morning light.

It's a time where our subconscious – full of the illogical thoughts and deeds we dare not act upon – flows into our conscious mind, much like a torrent of rapids heading for some great waterfall, unsuspecting and unprepared. We can no more stop it from happening as we can stop the waters from flowing over the falls and crashing unto the rocks below, nor should we. I am convinced that it is our dreams that give us a glimpse into the future, past, or perhaps both.

I believe that dreams guide us to where we should go, and our nightmares show us where we shouldn't. Through the years many great minds have tried to unlock the secrets of the dream world. Some say to understand the meaning of dreams is to understand one's soul. Don't know about that.

Others say dreams are the cause of déjà vu. When you think you recognize someplace you've never been or somebody you've never met, could you have actually been there and met that person in a dream you didn't remember? It's possible.

Dreams sometime show themselves during the day – reflected in the face of every young child. Dreams of lives not yet lived. Unlived and unrealized dreams are also reflected in the sad, graying eyes of the elderly, but not my dad's. Last month at age seventy-nine, he bought a house. He and his wife of nineteen years are going to move out of the condo. There'll be walls to paint, new furniture to buy, and a small garden in the side yard to tend. And there'll be something else: dreams once again in my father's sparkling blue eyes.

I have seen my share of dreams and my share of nightmares – some even of my own creation. Even so, I have never stopped dreaming and never stopped giving thanks. This Thanksgiving Day, I give thanks once more – for I indeed have much to be thankful for.

I look around and see my only son off at college and doing well – now sitting across the table from me eating his second piece of pecan pie. Around us – a brand new house built with love and care. We are all in good health. Our two cats run around inside, our big black lab lying in a wonderful backyard outside, and above all else – I see The Wife over there reading a book in a corner of the library built just for her. The Wife – a person I truly never dreamed I'd be married to. She is the person who's made all of my dreams a reality.

Early in the morning, when fingers of sunlight pry at your eyelids – wake up quickly – write down your dreams in that brief fleeting moment before they recede back into dreamland from whence they came. Once I did that, but not anymore. This Thanksgiving, the first of many in our new home, I can truthfully say that all of my dreams have now come true.

Mt. Olive Elementary School

You can't eat words. At least that's what Dad used to say when we were kids, but that's not what I remember. Growing up at 110 Flamingo Street, my brothers and I ate dirty words all the time. Usually the meal was accompanied by a couple of bites from a soap bar. Nowadays in the age of e-mail, text messaging, and video conversations, one must really be careful. There's no telling how hard it will be to consume a video.

Brain vs. Mouth

There are some things in this world I really don't understand. For example, why don't children (whatever their age) listen to their more mature, wiser parents? The Boy included. Why do lessons always have to be learned the hard way? Can't sometimes they be learned the easy way? And why is it that everything that tastes really good is full of calories and unhealthy? But what's at the top of my list? In the epic battle between brains vs. mouth, why does the mouth win every time? I have listed but a few of my classic gaffs to illustrate the point.

Old Mrs. Crabtree was my third grade teacher at Mt. Olive Elementary School. Every Monday, right after lunch, she'd list on the board twenty new vocabulary words that had to be memorized, defined, and used correctly in a sentence by Friday. It was two weeks before school was out for the summer, but she still wrote the list on the board anyway. Halfway through, she had to tell Bully Brad to stop talking. "Young man, we're not in this class to waste time."

That's when my brain stopped working and my mouth started. In my defense, it was right after lunch, the classroom was warm, and it was the end of the school year. The innocent little comment made under my breath changed my life, "Then why are we doing English?"

As she dragged me to the office by an ear, I heard laughter echoing down the hallway. It was at that moment I realized kids like a clown. Unfortunately, Old Mrs. Crabtree didn't, and she wasn't amused. She sentenced me to four days staying after school cleaning erasers. In this battle of brains vs. mouth, mouth had won.

By the tenth grade I'd gotten a little older and, one would think, a little wiser. This time the brainless mouth emerged again in Mr. King's algebra class. He had just written a long algebraic equation on the board, turned to the class, and said, "If a train left Chicago going 30 miles an hour and halfway through its trip was passed by a train from New York going 50, then what is X?"

At least that's what I heard as once again my brain disengaged and my big fat mouth engaged. At Briarwood High, home of the Mighty Buccaneers, shouting out answers was frowned upon. We first had to raise our hand, be called upon, and then respond. My hand shot up, I was acknowledged, and I proudly proclaimed, "If they took an airplane, they would get there faster. Besides, if X was so darned important, they would have found it by now."

The clown in me thought this response to be hilarious. Mr. King and Principal Baker both thought otherwise. Sweeping hallways after school for the next week, I had plenty of time to reflect on my response. Somehow, even in high school, it seems in the battle of brains vs. mouth, brain lost once again.

Lastly, the non-thinking mouth still gives me problems even today. When The Wife asks for my opinion of her outfit selection for the day, I give it. If a new rule is implemented at work, I'll immediately stop thinking and comment. And surrounded by a crowd whose members all have the polar opposite view politically than I, my mouth will be in overdrive without taking a single moment to think before speaking. But then again, how can a mouth actually think?

It's been a long time since I walked the hallowed halls of Briarwood, longer still since Old Mrs. Crabtree's third grade class. During the last eleven years of writing, I've learned that the pen is indeed mightier than the sword. And the unthinking mouth, at any age, will win the battle against brains every time.

At the end of one stressful day, I kissed The Wife and lay down to go to sleep. Three hours later, I resolved that sleeping wasn't going to happen, so I got up and wrote this story. I'm still trying to not stress as much, but like most things with me, it's a work in progress. Thankfully, I have The Wife's little foot to keep me in line when I stress too much.

Self-Induced Stress

It's difficult to be me. Trust me; I know. Sometimes I'm exhausted at the end of the day just from all the worrying. Some call it self-induced stress. I just call it worrying. And just when and where did all my worrying start you might ask? Well, none other than Old Mrs. Crabtree's third grade class at Mt. Olive Elementary School.

The location I'd picked out for my desk was not by accident. The third row over from the doorway and third seat back from the front was a strategic place – the direct center of the room. Not so close to the front that I'd be mistaken for a nerd – a real worry. And close enough to show Old Mrs. Crabtree that I was actually interested in what she had to say which of course I wasn't. Only a nerd would be.

The location of my desk was also the farthest away from my arch-nemesis Down the Street Bully Brad. Throughout third grade, Bradley McAllister hurled entire sheets of paper my way at least once a week in the form of spitballs. It wasn't a matter of "if," but "when." If I had known when, I wouldn't have worried so much. To this day, in any class I attend, the seat closest to the door is mine. That way an escape from any wet wad of paper from the back of the room can be made quickly.

Brad's still out there, and I never know when he'll show. The Wife and I went for ice cream last night, and I thought he was lurking in the shadows. Word has it he bought an ice cream store, but exactly where I don't know. See? Just something else for me to worry about.

Throughout Briarwood High, home of the Mighty Buccaneers, my worries continued. I worried whether Candi, my girlfriend since Mrs. Crabtree's class, would ever break up with Preston. She never did. It could've had something to do with Preston Weston being the richest kid who attended Briarwood and the fact I never informed her she was my girlfriend. I was always worried she would say no.

The worries I've had over the years, both large and small, have been too many to count. So many I've been promoted to the level of professional worrier. I heard that worrying can cause facial wrinkles. Thankfully for me, The Wife says she likes a wrinkly face.

Through my adult life, two other worries have been whether people like me and how I looked, but not anymore. I figure at age fifty-three if I'm not liked by someone, then it's their worry. And the way I look? Well, think about it, I don't really have to look at me, now do I?

Doctors say too much worrying can shorten your life. If that's the case, I should've been gone a long time ago. They also say eighty percent of what you worry about today is really nothing to worry about. Now all I have to do is figure out what twenty percent I do need to worry about.

When I told The Wife that I wanted to start a group for chronic worriers, she thought it was a great idea. Our motto can be "Don't be an amateur – let a professional worrier worry for you." If I started the club, I wonder if anyone would show up for the meetings. Great, now I have something else to worry about.

All my life, I've felt like a square peg trying to fit into a round hole. I was always trying to be someone else just to be considered cool. Now that I'm older, I finally realize that everyone feels like they don't fit in while they are growing up. If you're a square peg, all you have to do is find a square hole.

All the Cool Kids

All the cool kids do it. The first time I heard that phrase was in Old Mrs. Crabtree's third grade class. Ever since, I've been trying to be one of the cool kids. Why you may ask? The answer is simple. It's cool to be a cool kid. Unfortunately, I've always seemed to fall a little short when it came to the cool meter.

In the third grade, you were cool if you had a girlfriend. So I got one – and not just anyone. My girlfriend was the prettiest girl in all of Mt. Olive Elementary School. When Candi walked by, she'd take your breath away. You literally couldn't breathe. Guess it had something to do with the coconut conditioner she used and coconut perfume she wore.

All the way through third grade I knew I was cool because Candi was my girlfriend. Everyone else would have known too – if only I had told them. This, however, would have been hard – I didn't even tell Candi of her status until the fifth grade. So I guess I really wasn't cool after all.

Mrs. Crabtree's class wasn't my first ill-fated try at being one of the cool kids. Nope, the summer before that, you were considered cool if you could jump on a pogo-stick longer than anyone else. I quickly borrowed Preston's and started to jump. Preston Weston, III was the richest rich kid who lived over on The Duke of Gloucester. He was cool without trying to be cool. I guess rich kids were just destined to be cool.

After eight hours of jumping, I learned two things. First, jumping on a pogo-stick up and down Flamingo Street longer than anyone else in history really does make you cool. Second, all the coolness you gained from pogoing drains right out of your system if your brothers have to push you around in a wheelchair because your feet are so bruised you can't walk for two weeks.

My inability to become one of the cool kids followed me to Briarwood High, home of the Mighty Buccaneers. To be cool all you had to do was don the newest fad: a pair of bell-bottomed jeans. Now to many, this would seem a simple way to being cool, but again coolness escaped my grasp. To save money, Mom made our bell-bottoms.

She split our worn-out jeans from the knee down then inserted a piece of grandma's old kitchen curtains. For some reason, homemade bell-bottoms with yellow kitchen curtain inserts weren't considered cool way back then. There was one good side effect though: we never had to worry about our bell-bottoms getting stolen like the cool kids did. No one wanted them. And just for the record, because I know that bell-bottoms are now making a comeback, I'm telling all you moms out there – homemade bell-bottoms are still not cool.

Looking back at Mt. Olive Elementary, Briarwood High, and even my time spent at Auburn University, coolness eluded me. Luckily, about twenty-four years ago, that all changed. I became a firefighter. Now once every third day, the other vehicle I drive is a half-million dollar ladder truck. If that isn't cool, I don't know what is.

During our time spent growing up at 110 Flamingo Street, Dad gave sage advice about life that I still draw upon today. He told us never to quit. If life knocks you down, get back up. If you get knocked down again, then find another way, but don't ever quit. That advice is why this book has finally been published. I've been knocked down a lot since Flamingo Street. The picture on the back cover is proof, but I've always gotten up. And I've passed the same advice onto The Boy. I just hope he has listened.

Running Away From Fears

Few would disagree that everyone has a role to play in this life – even if that role is simply being a bad example for the rest of us. I believe we can learn more about ourselves when we try hard but lose than when we win. And if that's really true, then think of how much we could learn when we just up and quit, or better yet – when we run away. This story has its origin where many of my stories do – third row over, third seat back in Old Mrs. Crabtree's third grade class.

When I came home with a torn shirt, a bloody nose, and a black eye, Mom's reaction was predictable. She turned into a helicopter. Hovering over me before I could answer any of her twenty questions about what had happened to her darling little boy, the shirt was quickly removed, the bloody nose was wiped cleaned, and a cold compress was placed lovingly on my quickly swelling eye. When I told her what had happened, she hugged me and gave me a kiss on the forehead. It was the sweet kind of kiss that comes only from a mom – the kind that always makes everything better.

Now Dad – he was a different story, but his reaction was also predictable. It was once again lecture time. Why dads like to lecture so much, I don't know. Don't they know by now that kids don't listen to them? Err…except my son, The Boy. I'm sure he always listens to me when I lecture him.

"Winners never quit and quitters never win." That's what my Dad used to say whenever any of us kids wanted to give up at something – even if that something was a fight. "Stand and fight. You can't run away from your fears" was another one of his gems. Looking back, I see now that Dad's logic when it came to the topic of quitting or running away hasn't held up to the test of time. Heck, it didn't even hold up way back then – especially when it concerned Down the Street Bully Brad.

Bully Brad a.k.a. Bradley McAllister was my arch-nemesis the entire time we lived at 110 Flamingo Street. Every Friday after school, there was a fight down by the giant Magnolia tree in front of Candi's house. Mainly because that was as far as I could run before Brad caught up to me. He enjoyed the fights a lot more than I did. It became quickly apparent that it's better to be the beater than the beaten.

For thirty-five Fridays, the story was the same. I ran, he caught, he'd beat, I get beaten. By the thirty-sixth and last Friday of the school year, things had changed. Either I had gotten faster or all those extra sticky cinnamon buns Brad bullied people out of during lunch had finally slowed him down enough that I was able to outrun him. In either case, the times of Bully Brad chasing me down for a beating were finally over. Unfortunately the fights continued until we reached Briarwood High School, home of the Mighty Buccaneers; he just didn't run after me anymore.

It's been said that you learn all the important stuff about life while in the third grade. I don't know about that. Because during my third grade year in Old Mrs. Crabtree's class, the most important thing about life I learned was not while I was in third grade but out of it – specifically outside after school. You actually can run away from your fears. You just have to run really, really fast.

The Wife can look at any bad situation and find the good in it. When I was growing up at 110 Flamingo Street, Dad always said, "Out of everything bad something good comes. You just have to be able to see it." I'm extremely lucky –The Wife even sees being married to a reject as something good.

It's Hard Being a Reject

There comes a time in every person's life when they must accept who they are. I've finally arrived at that acceptance. After spending over two years behind the computer screen, my firefighter novel was finally finished and sent off to a big-time New York agent. One week later I received a very nice rejection letter by e-mail. I had The Wife read it, told her that I was a failure, and curled up in the corner and started to sniffle. She smiled, bent down, and gave me a hug, "Honey, you're not failure. You're just a reject."

The Wife has the amazing ability, no matter what the situation, to put a positive slant on things. We get a speeding ticket; at least we didn't wreck the car. Gas prices are at an all-time high; no problem - we need to walk more anyway. She has an extremely refreshing outlook on life. Unfortunately after two years of pounding away at the keyboard for hours each day only to be rejected, her positive outlook still eludes me.

My life as a reject really started in Old Mrs. Crabtree's third grade class. For the entire year, Candi Samples was my girlfriend. And I was going to tell her this fact in a note on the last day of school. Unfortunately, Mrs. Crabtree had a policy that if you were caught passing a note, you'd have to stand in front of the class and read it out loud. The note professing my love for Candi was intercepted by none other than Bully Brad.

Candi had no idea that I had feelings for her, but thanks to Brad, all of Mt. Olive Elementary School knew by the end of the day. I'm sure the fact that Preston Weston III, the richest kid in class who was already her boyfriend, really had nothing to do with her rejection of my offer. At least I think she rejected me. When I asked her after school to be my girlfriend, she couldn't stop laughing.

My being a reject didn't stop in elementary school. Briarwood High School, home of the Mighty Buccaneers, had tryouts for their new band when I was in the ninth grade. Girls love rock stars so I gave it a try and was rejected once again. Who knew that to be in a band you actually had to know how to play an instrument?

By the time I reached college, rejection and failure for me had become synonymous. After taking Physics 101 as a freshman, repeating it again as a sophomore and again as a junior, my career as an astronaut never got off the launching pad. Auburn University was really nice about it though. They sent me home for a semester to think about a new major and sent a letter to my parents.

Now, at fifty three, I've realized my dream of becoming an Olympic athlete is fading faster than my hairline. Being elected President of the United States is probably not going to happen either, and that may be a good thing. Considering what's happening in Washington, I really don't want any part of it. And it seems my career path of becoming the next John Grisham anytime soon has also been derailed by a nicely worded e-mail of rejection.

But even though the big-time NY agent took a pass on my book, I'm not giving up. I now proudly wear the banner of reject once again. Okay, I really don't wear a banner, but I did have several t-shirts made. So what do you do if you fail once or, like me, wear the t-shirt of a lifelong reject? Try, try again. At last count, there are 900 literary agents in the United States, which means I have only 899 more to go. One of them is bound to say yes to my novel. Even to a lifelong reject like me.

110 Flamingo Street

It's predicable. Anytime we're invited to a party, The Wife and I have the same conversation on our trip home. During the start of the trip, we'd agree how wonderful it would be to have a house full of our best friends over. They would enjoy one of our culinary dishes and sip some of our homemade adult beverages afterwards. Then we'd think about all of the work it takes to truly entertain. Luckily, by the time we've gotten home, we've talked ourselves out of entertaining altogether. Instead, we'll just go where we're invited and let our hosts do all the work.

The Anti-Socialite

Back when we lived at 110 Flamingo Street, Mom entertained all the time. It was actually only once a month, but to us kids that seemed like all the time. To say she was a socialite would be like BP saying, "Oops, we've spilled a little oil. Someone get a sponge." What an understatement! Mom was like Betty Crocker, Martha Stewart, and Paula Deen all rolled into one.

They say kids are a product of their parents. I really don't know who "They" are, but they're right. Watching Mom buzz around the house being a once-a-month socialite made me into the man I am today – an anti-socialite. What's the difference you may ask? It's simple: rules – lots and lots of rules.

The rules for being a socialite are far too numerous to list for just one column, so I'll concentrate on the most important. Those would be the ones Mom always followed. First and foremost: before any entertaining could take place, our house had to be cleaned from top to bottom. Now why my closet, under all our beds, and even the bathtub had to be cleaned I never could figure out. In the seven years spent at 110 Flamingo Street, not once were any of Mom's houseguests brave enough to venture into our bedrooms, much less rifle through our closets, and in spite of the tub's being cleaned by Scrubbing Bubbles, not one guest took a bath.

The second rule was similar to the first: all kids had to also be cleaned, and that meant even behind the ears. The reasoning behind this water torture was so we could meet the guests for all of ten seconds. The third rule was really Dad's rule: closing the bathroom door and running the water doesn't count as taking a bath or shower. One must actually enter the water, soap, rinse, and then repeat. This and only this would be considered bathing. And no, Dad didn't use Scrubbing Bubbles on us, but I'm sure he thought about it.

Next up, rule number four: the formal dining room was a "No Kid Zone" the day before and day of the dinner party. During this time, Mom rushed between the working in the kitchen, cooking enough food for an army, and making sure the long dining table was set correctly. By noon of the second day of our banishment, each place setting was flanked by spoons, knives, and three forks. Why three forks I really never found out. It may be because Big Steve from down the street was a regular guest and could eat three times as much as anyone else. Mom didn't let anyone go away from the dinner table hungry. And that was rule number five.

Being an anti-socialite is much simpler than being sociable and entertaining all the time like Mom. It's simple because there's only one rule to follow: there are no rules. Rooms don't have to be cleaned, multiple dirty rings are allowed (around tubs and children), and one fork is enough to down any meal. Betty, Martha, and Paula would disagree, but they're not anti-socialites like I am.

Besides, I've got a great idea for a new television show – *The Anti-Socialite Hour*. It could be the next number one hit! On second thought, having a hit television show really wouldn't work too well for me. I'm sure I'd have to take a bath every day and wash behind my ears.

Technology is so advanced now, some of us long for the good old days when things were less complicated and phones didn't come with instruction manuals the size of ...well...phone books.

Cups, String, and Dinosaurs

When Twin Brother Mark pulled the string tight and talked, I was blown away. With the can cupped to my ear, I heard everything he said. It didn't matter the span was only twenty feet between us and I could've heard him perfectly without the use of our new communication device. For us kids at the time, a soup can and string was the cutting edge of technology.

It has been said that animals that don't evolve will eventually become extinct. Dinosaurs are a good example. The mighty beasts that once thundered around the earth were at the top of the food chain, but something happened. Some scientists say the reason was a giant meteor crashed into the earth, blotting out the sun. The big creatures couldn't adapt to the rapid drop of temperatures and ensuing snowstorms. Others believe the dinosaurs simply ran out of food. Me? I just think they all were trampled to death. When it started to snow, there was a mass stampede to find the closest grocery store to get milk and bread. They all piled up in the parking lot and died.

A cup – a string – I was happy with that system. It was something everyone could understand and afford. We didn't need instructions printed in mice type and four different languages in order to know how things worked. Then again, Goofy Steve could have used some better instructions. He thought a full can of soup would work better than an empty can. After punching holes in the tomato soup can, he looked bloodier than he did after the Great Dirt Clod War of '69.

Long ago we moved away from 110 Flamingo Street leaving our tin cans and strings behind. It has been a struggle trying to keep up with the communication technology ever since. There seems to be no end in sight to the innovations. Like many older folks, I've tried to ride the crest of the new wave of gadgets. Unfortunately, last week the wave I was riding crashed headlong into rocks. The Wife and I got new cell phones. She has no trouble understanding the 150 different features of the one she got. I'm a lost ball in high weeds.

Fortunately, pulling me out of the wilderness was simple. I've learned early on in my adult life I don't have to be an expert at everything. I just have to know the person who is. To decipher the 150 different features on <u>my</u> phone, I called The Boy. He spent two years working at the big blue electronics store and knows a bunch about all that new fancy stuff. To be honest, I asked The Wife to call him. I still couldn't even find the power button.

The Boy spent the better part of a day trying to explain all the features of my new phone. The device had 3 gigs of storage capacity. I can text and surf the web at the same time. I can take pictures, movies, and notes. I even have a choice of over 1000 ringtones. To summarize: I held in my hand the latest and greatest communication device ever developed by mankind, a device that connected me to the world, and all for only $99 a month. Some innovation. The explanation of how to use Mark's can and string took less than a minute, and he had no monthly fees.

I smiled and said, "I just want a phone to sound like a phone." The Boy shrugged, changed my ringtone to actually ring like a phone and walked off. I think I heard him mumble something about a dinosaur. I couldn't have been happier and immediately called The Wife. I got her voice mail.

As with the tin cans and string from so long ago, all I want to do with my new phone is have the ability to talk to the person on the other end. I don't care if it has the ability to snap pictures, surf the web or take notes. That's why cameras, computers, paper and pencils were invented. When The Wife got home that night, I told her I didn't like my new phone. I longed for times gone by. She got up, got a blanket, and wrapped it around me. "It looks like snow. Here you go, dinosaur. This will keep you warm."

While taking the trash up to the curb one morning, I paused to view a rare sight. A green inchworm making its way up the gutter down spout – obviously completely lost. Why make such a climb I didn't ask. I don't speak inchworm. By the time I returned, the inchworm had made it to the top. I suddenly realized that even if you're lost, as long as you keep moving forward, you'll get wherever you're going – even if it's just one inch at a time.

Surviving Childhood

Long ago was truly a simpler time. It was a time of innocence. In my childhood, kids could just be kids. Our senses weren't bombarded by 24/7 news coverage of everything bad that happens in the world. We focused our attention on having fun. It's a time that has, unfortunately, forever passed.

With no bike helmets to protect us when we crashed, we simply hit the ground, rolled, brushed the dirt off, and got up to ride again. We had to. The bike helmet hadn't been invented yet. With three brothers to crash into, I crashed my bike quite often. Still, without a helmet, I survived. Although some would say evidence of all those crashes long ago is now starting to show.

When I was six, Mom wrecked our green station wagon with the faux wood brown panels. She spilt coffee on her lap and ran into a mailbox. After checking to see if we were injured, she grabbed some napkins and wiped up the spill. She didn't try to sue anyone because her coffee was too hot. Why would she? After all, coffee's supposed to be hot. When the police came, no ticket was issued because we weren't strapped in a child seat or restrained by seatbelts. Child seats hadn't been invented yet, and seatbelts weren't mandatory. Yet somehow we all survived.

No matter what happened to us, no matter how bad our situation had become, even when we thought the world and our lives were finally at an end, we survived. We always survived. And every morning the sun rose. It was like we got a whole new start on life. Mom used to say it was always darkest before the dawn. For many, this holiday season is getting really dark. It's all but festive. Some parents have lost their jobs, lost their homes, and have even started to lose the love they once had for each other. Some may say they're poor. I say they're rich.

They both still have the love of their children. And children can survive anything in childhood even without a helmet. As long as they know parents still love them back.

Take time, this holiday season, to show your kids you still love your spouse and them. They may never say it, but trust me, it's important. In troubled times it's easy to forget how much a miracle children really are. My sister and brothers knew we could survive anything because our parents would always be there for us. The love of a parent is the greatest gift you can give your child this Christmas – no matter how mature the child thinks they've become.

I told The Wife the other day that I felt like I've spent all my adult years being an inchworm, just inching along through life trying to survive, hanging onto one thin twig after another. Soon I'm going to stop all this inching. I'll simply turn into a butterfly and fly away. She smiled and said, "Honey, caterpillars turn into butterflies. Inchworms, when they grow up, get used for fishing bait."

Great. Who knew surviving childhood was the easy part of life? Surviving adulthood is proving to be quite difficult for this little inchworm. Thankfully, I married The Wife. She makes things so much easier. Just hope she doesn't get tired of my endless prattle and decides to use me for bait. And if she asks for a fishing pole for Christmas, I'll still stick around. I love her. Besides, even if I inch my way out of here as fast as I can, I wouldn't be able to go very far. 'Cause I'm an inchworm just trying to survive.

Break one of life's little rules and there are consequences to pay. It seems the older one gets the more rules there are, and the consequences are greater for the rule breakers. I learned early on in life, it's much easier to follow all the rules than to make up elaborate excuses why you didn't.

Rules of Life

There are rules of life everyone must learn – the easy way or the hard way. Looking back, I've learned most of them the hard way. I'm not proud of that fact, but a fact it still remains. Some of the most important rules of life I learned while residing at 110 Flamingo Street.

First rule: Don't be last in line for anything, especially if you're in trouble. All the good excuses will run out before it's your turn to lie. Case in point – an only child can do just about whatever they want because they have a perfect built-in excuse. If caught, they simply say, "Hey, I'm just a kid." A perfect excuse, yes, but since I had three brothers and one sister, Dad was tired of hearing it when he reached the end of the line and me.

By the time Dad got to me, all the good excuses were gone. The only thing I had was a blank look and the proverbial "I don't know." Trust me the "I don't know" thing doesn't work when priceless German crystal has been broken because of an indoor game of "Dodge-the-Frozen-Water-Balloon."

I also learned that being the last in line is not a good place when it comes to birthday cake or getting to the bathroom after all-you-can-eat taco night.

Rule number two: The "Hey, I'm just a kid" excuse doesn't work if you're not a kid anymore. This is really an important point for you youngsters out there. It doesn't work with girlfriends, wives, and certainly not that nice police officer at 3 a.m. – especially when you are being asked how fast you were going. That's not a life rule; it's a blue rule. And there's a bunch of those, but that's a story for another book.

Rule number three: Break one of life's little rules and there are consequences. Growing up at 110 Flamingo Street, there were consequences for not being able to come up with a good enough excuse. And usually the consequences came in the form of a thick black belt expertly wielded by Dad. Let's just say, with us five kids, he had a lot of opportunity to practice his belt-wielding technique. And by the end of the line, he was really warmed up.

Rule number four: Never forget an anniversary or birthday. Every time Dad did, he got into big trouble. The "I didn't know," "I'm sorry," or any other excuse won't work if you forget your loved one on that special day. Growing up, some of the biggest fights I can remember were when Dad forgot Mom's birthday or wedding anniversary. I don't know if she used a belt.

Lastly, Rule number five and perhaps the most important rule of all: Always tell the truth – especially if you're a terrible liar like me. My parents somehow always knew when I lied. They said it was written on my face. Every time I got caught, I'd looked in the mirror and not once did I see any writing. Funny how things change with time, but still stays the same. When The Boy was young, every time he lied, I could see it written all over his face. It must be a parent thing.

"Lying only makes things worse," my parents said. Some of the biggest whoopings were not because of what I did; it was because I had lied about what I had done. This rule is the same for the workplace – except when you lie at work, you don't get a whooping, you just get fired. The whooping comes when you go home and have to tell your better half. And yes, if you get fired for lying, the blue law is she gets to use a belt.

Mom and Dad

Every day I call my father. Some say I call out of duty. Others say it's out of love. Still others say I realize he has fewer days ahead than behind. If asked, I'd tell you it's a combination of all three and something else. I turned around one day, and Mom was gone. I realized then just how short our parent's lives really are. They sacrifice so much and their children don't realize it until they're gone. If it's Father's Day, call your dad; if it's Mother's Day, call your mom. Just call – while they're still able to answer.

A Nice Lady

I met a nice lady yesterday. She said she could type over 100 words per minute. While such a task is not so unusual in today's world of Twitter this and Twitter that, when she does, it is. She hugs her husband and then types – everything. Everything he says. She even types while hugging him. A strange relationship, for sure, but I guess it works for them. The happy hugging and typing couple have been married now for twenty years. They have five children.

I met a nice lady last week. She said she was very happily married to a wonderful, yet somewhat strange, man. He's a dreamer. Her feet are firmly planted on the ground. Over the years, he's written three books. All unpublished. His paintings fill the basement. To date, none have sold. And his inventions occupy every corner of their small country house. She's read his books multiple times. She's hung his paintings throughout their small house. And the inventions? Well, she still shows wonder for them – even though none actually works. The dreamer and realist have been happy together for thirty-one years.

I met a nice lady twelve years ago. She was the mother of two sons and two daughters, one of whom said yes when asked if she would marry me. The nice lady was so excited she never stopped talking. Then again, she has been gifted with the art of conversation all of her married life. Her husband is passionate about playing baseball. He's so good the coaches place him on teams with members ten years younger. And he still outplays all of them. She sits in the stands cheering him on, talking to anyone who will listen.

I think she constantly talks because she's so smart. I would have told her my theory, but she never took a breath. Her knowledge about the world is truly vast – so vast it can't be contained and just flows out.

He with his baseball and she with the art of conversation are truly a match. They have been together now for over fifty years.

I met a nice lady a long, long time ago. When I first saw her, she started to cry. For some reason our meeting had caused her a lot of pain. I tried to tell her that I was sorry. Sorry for hurting her, but it was as if we spoke a different language. She didn't understand me. Or maybe she did. For the more I talked, the less she cried. And eventually, slowly, a smile spread across her tear-streaked face. She stroked my hair and kissed my forehead as she held me close counting my fingers and toes. She whispered in my ear, "Don't cry little one. It'll be okay. I love you."

I decided to stay with that nice lady and her man. I enjoyed their company for the next twenty-four years. I guess they enjoyed mine. They let me stay. We were together up to the day that nice lady left. Her man cried for weeks. I tried to comfort him, but again, it was as if we spoke a different language. How could someone twenty-four possibly understand a partnership that had lasted over thirty-three years? It was a great loss to us both. I've recovered somewhat. He was changed forever that day and has never been the same.

Gifted with conversations, tolerant with the oddities of life, or simply the love of someone's life – moms are all different yet all the same. My advice to you this Mother's Day is simple. Visit the nice lady who sacrificed so much for you through the years. Give her a hug and say thank you. Though not a pleasant thought, she will not be around forever. What I wouldn't give for one last hug from that nice lady I met many years ago. And to hear her voice once again whisper in my ear, "Don't cry little one. It'll be okay. I love you."

Some of my fondest memories of childhood are of the holiday season and its many traditions: stringing lights on the tree, draping the Sister with tinsel, and throwing ornaments at my brothers. Somehow, we all came together and stopped fighting long enough to help Mom with the cards. A tradition I've tried to keep alive with The Boy.

The Christmas Card

Funny thing about life is that if you live long enough, you'll have the chance to play each role. To better illustrate my point, we'll use one of the many traditions of the season – the Christmas card. Since its Christmas Eve, one would think great thought and timing went into this article. Nope, I just needed a break from writing all of those addresses. I finished mine in ten minutes, but The Wife's got lots and lots of friends and needed some help.

Growing up at 110 Flamingo Street, weeks before the real tree went up in the family room and the fake white tree went up in the living room, Mom would start the business of sending Christmas cards. For two weeks out of the year, our dining room table was converted into an assembly line. At one end would be the huge stack of store-bought cards. We watched as Mom took great pains to write a special note on each one and then address the envelope before it was sent down the line where it was stuffed, licked, stamped, and eventually stacked. For the ones going to kids, there would be an extra stuffing. Mom always stuffed the envelopes with five $1 bills.

We all had a role to play in the assembly. Big Brother James was the stuffer. Twin Brother Mark and I used a wet sponge to seal the envelopes. Of course, that was after we licked the first ten or so. By then, we had decided that the reality of not getting into trouble for sticking our tongues out at The Sister all afternoon wasn't as fun as it sounded.

Older Brother Richard was the lone stamp affixer, and The Sister was the stacker. Every year Mom had us rotate so we could learn each position. It kept down on some of the fighting that way. Besides, one day we would have kids and how would they learn if we didn't rotate and learn each position?

Through it all, we listened to Mom describe about when she was young and about how different things were way back then. "We didn't send store-bought cards; they were too expensive. My mom had us kids make all the Christmas cards. That's what made them special."

Even to this day, I can still remember how archaic I thought a homemade card was. It wasn't until many years later, when The Boy was five, that I finally realized my folly. Having children changes everything – even the way you perceive the business of sending Christmas cards.

I remembered what Mom had taught us kids, the stories of when she was a little girl, and how much fun she had making cards. So two weeks before Christmas, I converted the dining room table into an assembly line and decided to carry on the tradition of card-making with The Boy. Store-bought cards were replaced with construction paper, glitter, and glue. After the first week, I too understood just why Mom used store-bought cards with us.

This year, the business of sending Christmas cards has changed for me once again. Slow, archaic hand addressing was replaced with the speed of a computer mail merge that printed directly onto the envelopes. Hand stuffing, sponge sealing and stamp licking still had to be done though, but it didn't take long. On the way to the post office, proud of my card accomplishment, I phoned The Boy and described how what used to take two weeks now took less than three hours. Surprisingly, he laughed.

"Dad, that's the old-fashioned way. All you had to do was send the computer files to the drug store. They would've done all that addressing, sealing, and stamping, and mailing."

"Aha, yes!" I answered. "But you're forgetting the most important thing – the extra stuffing. I guess this means you don't want the twenty dollars I stuffed into your envelope?"

Pulling into the post office parking lot, I hung up the phone and smiled. The Boy, I think he's starting to see the value of doing Christmas cards the old-fashioned way.

New moms develop super hearing the moment their babies are born. They can hear them cry from all the way across the house. This super hearing only heightens as the child gets older. Kids, be careful what you say, even when you don't think your mom is listening. You can't eat words, but trust me, you may eat a bar of soap if the words you say are bad ones. And if you're wondering, I never won a debate with Mom on whether a word was a bad one or not. And The Boy hasn't won that argument with me either.

The Court of Mom

Watch what you say. It can and will be used against you in the Court of Mom. There is an old saying "Think before you speak." And like many old sayings, it provides sage advice. But over the years I've learned something extremely important. If you have to think about what you're about to say, it's probably in your best interest not to say it. What's the worst thing that could happen if you chose to say what's on your mind anyway? Trust me, any repercussions at work will pale in comparison to what could happen to you if you say the wrong thing to your Mom. Biting a bar of soap and getting your mouth washed out is something you want to avoid at all cost.

Growing up at 110 Flamingo Street, not a week went by without one of us four boys being marched into the bathroom. When Mom deemed what we said to be a bad word, biting the bar of Ivory soap and getting our mouth washed out was our punishment – an action, I might add, that in today's society should be outlawed. And when we switched from Ivory soap to that multi-colored Irish Spring, it could've been considered almost as bad as water-boarding.

In Old Mrs. Crabtree's third grade class, if you wrote something down, at least you had a chance to erase it before she saw it. Talking is different. Once you say the wrong thing, bad words can't be taken back. You can't eat words. Unless of course they're written down and you can't erase them fast enough. Believe me, an entire sheet of notebook paper full of bad words, when crumpled and crammed, will fit into the mouth of a ten-year-old.

As radical as it may seem, this action did accomplished three things. First, it was a good way to destroy all the written evidence of anything that Mrs. Crabtree might have considered bad or offensive.

Second, it staved off another trip to the office and a visit with Principal Baker. Third, and perhaps most importantly, the entire sheet of notebook paper filled with bad words crammed into the mouth made for one heck of a mega spitball – perfect to throw at Down the Street Bully Brad when he least expected it.

One very important note for all you parents out there – Hell is not a bad word. It is a place. That's why it capitalized. Just ask Mrs. Newsome my tenth grade English teacher at Briarwood High, home of the Mighty Buccaneers. (Of course, if you ask The Boy, that place was our home during his teenage years.)

The worst mouth-washing I received was when I tried to debate my mom on the hellish issue about Hell. Our debate came to a head one Sunday morning when Preacher Jim was in rare form. By the end of the preaching hour, he was red faced and sweating.

I guess it was all that talking about Hell that got him so hot. After the service, Preacher Jim greeted us at the door and asked, "Did you enjoy the sermon, young man?"

I answered, "Well, Hell, yeah." That's when Mom tried to pull me away by one ear. She said we were going straight home and a certain someone was going to get his mouth washed out with soap. I thought she was talking about Preacher Jim. Fair was fair. He had said Hell more times in the past hour than I had in the last year. It didn't help my case much that I made the suggestion when we were standing right in front of him.

It has been said that we have two ears and one mouth for a reason. We're supposed to listen twice as much as we speak. Sounds like really good advice – especially if you're in the Court of Mom. Besides, no one has ever gotten sick from having his ears washed out with soap.

The Wife and I live in a small Southern town steeped in a rich history – and we try to take the time to see it. This vacant lot is still there, with the tree in front of the crumbling foundation. Sometimes we have to look back to see where we've been in order to know where we're going.

The Tree

Some in the town say the tree has stood for a hundred years. Others say it's much older. Alone in a field of emerald grass almost as soft as carpet, the old pear tree still stands – although it has seen better days.

It was magnificent; its branches once reached thirty feet towards the sky, but no longer. Bent and twisted by time and circumstance, what's left of the largest pear tree in town now barely reaches one-third that height. Still, against all odds, from season to season, its function hasn't changed: providing shade from the harsh sun during the summer and fresh fruit during the fall.

In front of the small clapboard house they erected at the edge of the Southern town, loving newlyweds had planted the sapling. She was expecting the first of their five children; he was commemorating the moment of homeownership…and fatherhood – both of which excited and frightened him. As their family grew, so did their love for each other.

The tree also grew. It bore fruit the second year. This was unusual for a pear tree, but this was to be no ordinary tree. During the spring, it provided pink fragrant blooms. Late in summer, the branches hung heavy with fruit – firm and juicy – perfect for pies and canning. During the winter, the hairnet of branches provided a barrier against the frigid northern wind. By the fourth year, its branches were strong enough to support a climber. And the first of their children became one.

In their time, each of the five children followed suit, and so did the grandchildren. The giant pear tree welcomed them all. During the Great Depression, it provided an abundance of fruit for the family, both for canning and for selling. So much so they were able to hold onto their home when many others were losing theirs.

In '69 the small clapboard house caught fire. Luckily, the entire family got out safely and met at their special place so the father could account for everyone. The meeting place was under the grand old pear tree in the front yard. Unfortunately, the house was a total loss. The heat damaged the tree so badly that many limbs were scorched and had to be cut, yet it still survived. The very next year, it bore fruit. After all, what good to anyone is an old pear tree that isn't productive?

Instead of rebuilding, the family moved into a new modern subdivision on Flamingo Street but still came by to visit the tree and enjoy the pink fragrant blooms in spring and harvest its fruit in the fall. That was until two years ago. A horrific storm passed through the now bustling town, uprooting most of the old trees. It took six months for the loggers to cut all the fallen trees and clear all the lands, but no one touched the old pear tree – it had survived the storm – but again, not unscathed. A stray lightning bolt had arched across the blackened sky that night, struck down half the tree, and in doing so, sealed its fate. It's well known that once a tree is struck, it will not survive.

Last week I stood below the tree and filled a bag full of pears. In a year, maybe two, the end will come and it will bear fruit no longer. I gazed at its twisted form, found the foundation of the old clapboard house and was quickly overcome with emotion. This once majestic tree that so many had depended upon through the years was now a mere shadow of what it once was. It saddens me still.

The fruit we bear comes back to us over time. Some years we have a better harvest than others. The ripe old age of eighty-three is a milestone not many reach. And those that do reach it have been bent and twisted by not only time, but also by circumstance. Just like the old pear tree, they are magnificent because they still bear the fruit of wisdom, knowledge, and love.

Happy Birthday, Dad. Thanks for still being around and bearing fruit.

When I became a dad, suddenly I realized quickly that children don't come with instructions. Parents do the best they can when they raise their children. Some do better than others, but none are really prepared for the job. Thankfully, most still have parents they can call on for advice. It's amazing how much smarter our parents become as we get older. They still have a lot to give, if we only take the time to listen.

Everyday observations have been, and will continue to be, the inspirations for many of my stories. Just like this one.

This Old Man

In the brightly lit washroom, there was one lonely attendant, an old man, somewhat hunched over with age. When I saw him, he was holding a fresh towel with one hand and a small broom and dust pan on the end of a stick in the other. Eyes fixed on the ground directly in front of his tattered shoes, in his mind he was someplace else. It was Father's Day.

The attendant handed a towel to the gentleman who had just emerged from one of the three stalls in the upscale washroom. In return he gave the old man two dollars. Slowly he stuffed the bills into the right pocket of his worn gray suit coat with patches on the sleeves. The old man nodded in gratitude. The gentleman left the washroom without giving the attendant who stood in the corner another thought. Much like one would not give a second thought to a chair that had served its purpose or an emptied drink can tossed out the window of a fast moving car.

Rubbing his salt and pepper whiskers with his right hand, the attendant walked over and cleaned the stall vacated a moment earlier, then returned to his corner in the washroom. He stood just left of the sinks, next to the two-chair shoe shine stand. A smile cracked his face. It was a smile of weary acceptance.

It was Father's Day once again, and once again he was alone.

I wondered what sad turn of events had led to the old man ending up as an attendant in an upscale washroom. Was it by necessity or by choice? Had the meek, quiet man in the corner bent by time and circumstance actually lived a full happy life and now this was his only contact with the outside world? Was he to wind up like the drink can – tossed out the window when he had nothing else to offer?

It was Father's Day, and he was alone. His children had forgotten again.

Your parents are the people that have been constant in your life as far back as you can remember. They've guided you growing up and gave you advice about the important stuff – whether you wanted it or not.

In kindergarten Dad told me not to eat Play-Doh. Good advice. At the start of the fifth grade, Dad taught me how to defend myself against bullies. This was timely advice. Down the Street Bully Brad was in my classroom that year.

At the start of high school, Dad encouraged his four children to get involved with athletics. He said it would help to teach us life lessons. Some lessons were harder to learn than others. Glad I wore a helmet.

In real life there're no helmets to protect you, but there's always your dad. In the tenth grade Dad read my report card and said I could do better. I started to study, and two years later I was accepted to Auburn University. Dad's advice paid off. It often has over the years.

Now, with his job done, your father has but one question still left unanswered. How did he do in raising you? This Father's Day give your father what he really wants – an answer to that question. Sit down with him and tell him just how great a job he really did. And bring the grandkids. He can advise them not to eat Play-Doh. Still sound advice even today.

Back in that upscale washroom, it was time to go home. The washroom attendant stored his unused towels, broom, and dust pan on the end of a stick in a closet just outside and locked the door. The old man shuffled through the crowded food court, past the hamburger stand, past the baseball memorabilia shop, and past the chocolate shop. He stopped at a bench in front of the arcade.

Slowly, he sat down. As the children visiting the arcade gathered around, he reached into his torn coat pocket and started to give out dollar bills. They knew his routine. It was the same routine he's repeated every Father's Day for the last ten years. This old man still had a lot of love to give. So does your dad. Don't call him on Father's Day. Go see him. Tell him you appreciate all of his advice over the years and how through it all, you still love him. Tell him that now you don't only see him as a dad, but as a person. A person you'd like to get to know better. It will be the second best gift he ever got for Father's Day. The first, of course, was you.

The Boy

The month before The Boy went off to college, I tried to have one last father/son talk. The more I talked, the more he ignored me. After ten minutes, I became frustrated and simply gave up. I closed his door, walked down the steps, and suddenly realized I knew what my father felt some thirty years earlier when he walked away from my door.

Dependently Independent

There's a place where facts, myths, and legends merge – blending together in our minds into a soft, purple, swirling haze. It's a place where each of us was the star, the captain of the football team, the head cheerleader, the smart kid with the 4.0 average, or the popular kid that everyone wanted to be and be seen with. Memories. Somehow, now that we have children of our own, we've forgotten the awkwardness of adolescence as it slowly ebbs away with time. In time, we have forgotten how hard it actually was.

Things that we once lived and died for (hanging out at the mall with our friends, talking endlessly on the phone about everything and nothing, dating that someone we knew our parents didn't approve of just because they didn't approve of him or her and just because we could) don't seem as important to us any more as we're burdened with the everyday responsibilities of being adults. Back then, we did everything we possibly could to push the limits of their tolerance with our risky behavior for no other reason than just to see how far it would stretch. But those same things are still important to our kids: acknowledgment, acceptance, and above all else – being dependently independent.

Memories. The more time passes, the more perfect we were as teenagers. We were teenagers who never gave our parents any trouble, and if we did, somehow we remember that it was <u>they</u> who did not understand our wants or needs. <u>We</u> did not misunderstand their responsibility to set down rules to raise their children in accordance with societal norms so we could be a success in school and later in life. Upon seeing our children's report card, instantly we reinvent memories, making us smarter than we actually were in high school or college – conveniently forgetting all the bad quizzes and test grades that were handed back to us while we daydreamed in math class. The math class we barely received a passing grade in.

Memories make us more popular than we actually were in college and help us forget how much our parents helped us out when we were still looking for our first job and a place to live. And with time, the line between what really happened in our youth and what we wish happened gets blurred. Our perspective gets skewed.

All our children want is food, a dry roof over their heads, an allowance, and love when they seek it. But for the most part they just want to be left alone. Face it: parents are the stupidest people who've ever walked the face of the Earth. What could a teenager possibly learn from someone who is so old and so clueless? If we search our memories – our real memories – it's the same thing we thought about our parents but didn't dare to articulate. It was a different time, but the same time.

So as we walk away, we leave our kids in their rooms behind closed doors. There, they'll talk endlessly on cell phones until all hours of the night or play video games over the internet against their friends in another neighborhoods or watch TV or plan what party they will go to and with whom. As good parents we leave them alone. They don't have time to talk to us anymore. They don't understand that the time they can spend with us is coming rapidly to a close. We leave them alone, for a very good reason. So they can be dependently independent.

Every May and June kids around this country graduate from high school. The very next month parents will help them pack, then drive them to college. Where instantly, and here's the tricky part, they're supposed to act like adults. There they will stay. And teary-eyed parents will drive back – alone. Our children have memories of their own to create. And later recreate…when they have children.

The teenage years. Wow! Having gone through them, I truly understand why babies are made so cute and cuddly. It's so you'll fall in love with them. That way, when they become teenagers, you won't just move away while they're off at college without giving them your forwarding address. Not that I'm admitting to anything, mind you, but The Boy eventually did find us. It took his entire Christmas break, but he found us.

Behind Closed Doors

A person much smarter than me once said, "A man is not measured on how he starts things. He is measured on how he finishes them." How true and how timely – for we just dropped The Boy off at college today. He starts down the road of higher education, a road that will have many twists and turns. Waiting for him at the end are a college degree, possibly a wife, and the maturity that only four more years of studying will bring. These are the years that will test his strengths and weaknesses and eventually make The Boy into a man.

We wish him the best of luck, but a few times over the last year I really didn't think he'd make it. To be quite honest – I really didn't think I would either.

The Boy, like most teenagers, has spent the better part of the last year at our house up in his room with the door closed. He has come down only for the briefest of times for life's necessities: to grab food and drink, to use the bathroom or take an occasional shower, and to argue with his dad. There have been lots of those of late – arguments that have become louder and more frequent as the time for his departure drew closer.

He sat behind his closed door watching television, playing video games, working on his computer, or chatting endlessly on his cell phone with his friends. They too sat behind their closed doors. He sat behind his closed door hiding from the world. He sat behind his closed door hiding from his father who in the last year has somehow become the stupidest man on the planet and his favorite target for endless, senseless arguments. Arguments about everything and nothing. Arguments with a father who, of late, has been the impediment to his growing up. Arguments that wasted the precious time they had left together.

The Boy sat behind his closed door, hiding from himself, while at the same time trying to find who he really is.

After dropping him off at school, The Wife and I returned back home at about two in the afternoon, plenty of time to still get in a half day's work. We have four years of college to start paying for. But before I get started – before I get on with the rest of my life – there is something important I must do.

Walking up the stairs to The Boy's empty room, I remember. I remember how small he was the first time I saw him in the hospital. I remember the first time he said "Dad, I lobe you." I remember his first taste of Co-Cola and the funny face he made as the bubbles tickled his nose.

I remember how, when he finally caught that elusive blue tail lizard, he screamed as its tail fell off (a defense mechanism used to get away from the excited grasp of little boys). I remember another scream, one of pain, as the baby snapping turtle clamped down and wouldn't let go of a curious little finger that got too close. I remember Little League baseball games and waiting for him through high school football practices that went well into the night, practices that helped to temper The Boy and started him well onto his way to becoming a man.

I remember the divorce that almost tore my soul apart and the look on his tear- stained, crestfallen face as I drove away. I remember two years later how he chased the parachute from a rocket shot so high into the sky that it almost disappeared from sight. That was the first meeting between him and his soon-to-be stepmom. When asked later that night what he thought of the lady he had shot rockets off with in the high school parking lot, he replied with a smile on his face, "Dad, I like her; she's funny." The Wife and I were married three months later. The Boy was the proudest usher in the church.

As I close the door to his room, I remember every bit of our eighteen short years together. All the good and all the bad. It seems it was just yesterday that I held him for the very first time in my arms. When he looked up at me with those clear blue eyes, the memories started – memories that to this day have never stopped.

I close the door to his room and slowly turn away. That way, for the next few years, whenever I pass the stairwell and glance up, I can imagine The Boy still up there. Hiding behind that closed door. Trying to find himself. Hopefully it will help to muffle the emptiness I now feel inside as the echoes of the memories of him and our life together flow down the steps, reverberate through the hallway, and engulf each room with the sadness of a time that will never come again.

A time gone forever – kept alive now only in memories.

Becoming an adult means having new responsibility. And becoming a new homeowner means having a lot of new bills. A year after this story was written, The Boy finally saved enough to purchase his washer and dryer. It was a year later when he finally realized that to wash something red with something white means to wear pink underwear.

Who's This We, Kemo Sabe?

Last week The Boy closed on his first house. He's all moved in and enjoying home ownership somewhere amongst all the boxes. As he surfaced for air, reality finally set in. A few "must have" things didn't come with his house. So he did what anyone in his situation would do. He made a phone call. "Dad, we have a problem. What are we going to do about a washer and dryer?"

To quote Tonto from the Lone Ranger, "Who's this WE, Kemo Sabe? We have owned a washer and dryer for the last thirty years. I believe it's you that has a problem. And I have the perfect solution."

The Boy listened attentively to what came next. He thought the perfect solution was obvious. We, The Wife and I, would be forking over money for his new washer and dryer. Boy, was The Boy wrong! Instead of money, he got the following story and an invaluable life lesson.

Growing up, Preston Weston III lived over on The Duke of Gloucester. The Duke, as we who lived on Flamingo Street called it, was where all the rich families lived. And Preston's family was one of the richest. Rumor was that his dad either invented Silly Putty or was a spy. Never did find out which. Either way, whatever Preston wanted, Preston got.

Preston was the first on The Duke and Flamingo to have a three-speed bike and the first kid to fly in an airplane. I think it was his dad's spy plane. Preston never said it was, which meant that there was a good chance it was a spy plane or it was made of Silly Putty. Looking back, I know now that it was ridiculous to think so. Preston's dad could never be a spy.

In the ninth grade, Preston tried out for the Buccaneers. He was the only ninth grader ever to start at quarterback. Coach Reeves played him every game, and he set all kinds of school records. At the end of the season, the Buccaneers got new pads, game jerseys and a new locker room.

Anything Preston needed while attending Briarwood was provided. If he fell behind in his studies, private tutors were at his house the next day. When Preston tried out for the basketball team, his dad bought him fifty-dollar shoes. Now who in their right mind would buy their kid a pair of fifty dollar basketball shoes? Preston wore them once and decided he didn't want to play basketball. He ran track instead.

Preston was also the only student at Briarwood that was on the varsity track team for five straight years. He was the high jumper. High jumpers have special shoes that make them jump higher and Preston's dad bought one. He would have bought two, but Preston only jumped off the right foot. The man was smart; he invented Silly Putty.

At the end of the story, The Boy said, "So whatever Preston wanted all he had to do was ask his parents and they gave it to him. Sounds like a good idea. I bet if he asked for a washer and dryer they would have bought them for him."

"Probably so, but he wouldn't have appreciated all the hard work it took to earn the money to buy them." I gave him direction to the nearest all night laundromat.

The Boy mumbled under his breath as he emptied his change jar, "Thanks, Dad, for the invaluable life lesson." At least I think that's what he said.

The Wife

During spring, The Wife spends a week going through the house boxing up all of the junk we gathered throughout the past year. Afterwards, it never ceases to amaze me how much bigger our house looks and feels. Now if only I can find my cell phone. I think it's in one of those boxes I took to the basement.

This story is my mother-in-law's favorite and for good reason. It seems growing up, The Wife was a minimalist at her house also.

The Minimalist

"For richer or poorer, in sickness and in health, for better or worse...." Those were the marriage vows I took. No one said anything about becoming a minimalist. If they did, I would have remembered it. Don't know what a minimalist is? Me neither – had to look it up.

As I was coming in from cutting grass, the Wife met me in the kitchen. She said, "Honey, I think I'm becoming a minimalist."

As I poured a glass of water, I replied knowingly, "Okay." Then put the water pitcher back into the refrigerator, but not before spilling some on the floor. I reached for the roll of paper towels, but they weren't on the counter top. In fact, there was nothing on any of the kitchen counters.

Following me into the bathroom she asked, "You don't know what a minimalist is, do you?"

"Nope, not a clue," I retrieved a bath towel and started back to the kitchen, "Don't even know where the paper towels are."

"A minimalist is someone who doesn't like to have everything out on display. A true minimalist will have only one or two things per shelf, very few pictures on the walls, and nothing on counter tops. What do you think about that?"

Bending over to clean up the water I replied, "At least now I know what happened to the paper towels."

"No...really, what do you think?"

Tossing the towel towards the laundry basket and missing, I shrugged, "I think you've watched too much HGTV." Note to all you Neanderthals out there: shrugging at your wife doesn't help to foster a loving relationship. The shrug and comment earned me a punch in the arm.

For the next twenty minutes, The Wife took me around the house and proudly showed off her minimalism. Countertops, desks, night stands, dressers and shelving were completely clear of junk – mostly my junk. The entire house had been de-cluttered. I must admit, our house did look neater... and bigger. Get rid of all the junk, and the house will double in size. Guess we really didn't have to move after all.

Even the bathrooms had not survived her minimalist culling. On my side of the bathroom the only things left out were a toothbrush, soap, and a box of tissue. Gazing over at The Wife's side, things were vastly different. A pear shaped bottle of perfume, half a dozen knick-knack boxes, a vase of flowers, and a silver canister of small paint brushes adorned her counter.

When asked where everything went, The Wife replied, "The things we didn't need and weren't essential are now boxed up and in the basement."

I pointed towards her counter, "But all your make-up stuff is still out."

"That's because makeup is essential."

Not wanting to argue, or get punched in the arm again, I spent the rest of the day in the basement – sorting through all of my "non-essential" stuff. My collection of miniature bath soaps, shampoos, conditioners, hand creams, and shower caps – all procured from places we stayed while on vacation the last eight years – filled two of the boxes. How they could be categorized as "non-essential" was beyond me.

Two other boxes contained stuff from The Boy's room. He's off at college, and we're turning that room into an office. At least last time I talked to him he was at college. He only calls when he needs money, or when he...well...needs money.

The last box was filled with flower vases, pictures that never got hung on the walls, and the old toaster oven. After two hours, I finally had enough.

I was not going to give in to The Wife. Even if she was a minimalist, I didn't have to be. If I wanted all my stuff lying out everywhere, then so be it! I put my foot down, unboxed all of my non-essential things, and proudly displayed all of them back on shelves where they belonged. I felt like the man of the house once again. Then I cut off the light and left the basement.

Meeting her in the kitchen I said, "Hey, I finally know what minimalism is."

"What is it?"

"It's when you get tired of all my stuff lying around so you box it up and throw it in the basement. Guess there's nothing I have that is worthy of staying upstairs."

As I pouted, The Wife walked over and tugged at my shirt. Then she looked up and gave a conspiratorial smile. As she winked and kissed me, she said, "No dear, there are a few things you have that are essential. And they can stay upstairs."

This story happened just as written. Due to the space afforded in the newspaper for my column, a few events of the day were omitted. We watched homemade ice cream being churned by a small motor mounted on a miniature tractor. It was the best ice cream either of us had ever eaten. We bought honey from a beekeeper that had been stung over a hundred times but still loved raising bees. We petted giant chickens and enjoyed watching one of the state's largest Memorial Day parades. In all, it was one of those days a couple looks back on and smiles.

True Price of Air-Conditioning

The Wife just stood there. First she giggled; then she started to laugh. And for a change, the laughter wasn't directed at me. Her mirth was in response to what I thought was a simple question. "Where did the large black spot on the inside of the bedroom dresser drawer come from?" The answer she finally gave was so unique it had to be true. It was a tar ball stain. But that's the end of the story. Here is the beginning.

Like most, The Wife and I enjoyed the holiday together. We watched our small town's parade and afterwards snaked our way through the various venders who seemed to occupy every square inch of shade beneath the giant oak and pecan trees scattered around our downtown square. At about three in the afternoon, after viewing the fourth table loaded down with homemade soap, my fun meter was pegged out. It was time to escape the heat. The Wife took my arm and led me into a large furniture store for some refuge and much needed air-conditioning. Note to all you Neanderthals out there: if this ever happens to you, go the other way. Your refuge is about to get expensive.

Upon entering the store, we were met by a blast of cool arctic air and the warm smile of a saleslady. They talked while I sank into the most comfortable loveseat on the planet. Unbeknownst to me, it was the very loveseat that The Wife had picked out last weekend. And yes, I agreed that it was a "must buy." Besides, the thing was so soft I couldn't get out of it to put my foot down and say no. But the story is just getting started.

It seems that the throw pillows on the loveseat magically matched the chair in the window that The Wife fit so nicely into. Throw pillows are just that – pillows you throw onto other furniture for no other reason but to make people buy more furniture while they are enjoying air-conditioning on one of the hottest days of the year. It was decided that the incredibly soft loveseat, chair, and matching throw pillows would not see another day in that store.

Looking back, it's possible that that nice saleslady and The Wife had a master plan to redecorate our master bedroom. When asked, The Wife just smiled, helped me up, and off to pay we went. And, to be truthful, we would have a lot more money left if I hadn't sat down...again.

The nice saleslady asked us to sit in the two chairs next to her desk while she wrote up delivery papers. I'm a sucker for a chair that swivels. And the cute chairs not only swiveled, they also rocked. I swiveled, rocked, spun, and apparently answered each question asked by the saleslady with a grin and a nod. After ten minutes, we had not only agreed to an additional buy of the chairs, but also paid for fabric coating, delivery, and I think her next vacation home. An hour after we entered the air-conditioning, we were set free and sent back into the blast furnace. But I didn't really care. We were getting swivel chairs. And by "we," I mean me.

Once home we had to move the antique dresser out of the master bedroom to make room for the new loveseat. Where else in the house would you place a loveseat other than the bedroom? The Wife has had the dresser since she was six years old. I started to unpack the drawers when the discovery of the childhood stain was revealed. As a little girl, she was fascinated by newly tarred streets. When summer day temperatures are in the mid-nineties, tar starts to turn soft. It seems that The Wife used to make tar balls to play with, just like me and my brothers did when we lived at 110 Flamingo Street. And she kept them around for the same reason we did: Sisters really don't like tar balls – especially when you put them in their underwear drawer.

Cape or no cape, there's a little of Captain Obvious in each of us, but beware! Not everyone appreciates the superhero powers of the Captain – especially if you happen to be married.

Captain Obvious

Some superheroes are born out of necessity; others have heroism thrust upon them. Captain Obvious didn't arrive from a distant plant, spring forth from the molten core of the earth, or cross over from a parallel universe. On New Year's Eve he was born out of what seemed to be a benign statement made by yours truly: "Honey, you know tomorrow is New Year's Day."

The Wife, as lovable as she is, could not let the comment go unanswered. "Thank you, Captain Obvious." It's a moment that will go down in superhero history. Now that I've officially dubbed myself a superhero, I must spend my days doing superhero stuff – like pointing out all the obvious things people do.

Announcing that the phone is ringing was the first job for Captain Obvious. Stating the trashcan under the kitchen counter was full or that someone needed to unload the dishwasher were two others. Rolling over at 3am and muttering that the dog is barking and needs to go out was also a job for Captain Obvious. Unfortunately, actually taking the dog out was too. And take it from me, long-johns or no, it was downright cold out there.

After just one week of living with a superhero, The Wife wanted to change my name to Captain Obnoxious. Undeterred by the not-so-welcome welcome Captain Obvious had received at his hidden hideaway, he ventured out into the world to the local coffee shop. After giving my order, I pulled around to the window and announced, "You know the drive-thru is only for those people who don't want to get out of their cars." Driving off, I just knew they appreciated the wisdom bestowed upon them by Captain Obvious.

The guys I work with at the fire department didn't really care much for the Captain. It seems they didn't need him to tell them the phone was ringing, to instruct them to go on calls after they had been dispatched over the radio, or to announce at 2am that it was really cold outside. Sometimes even a superhero doesn't get any respect.

It was then I realized that to be taken seriously, I needed a costume. Asking The Wife for help designing Captain Obvious's costume didn't work too well. She couldn't stop laughing. Finally catching her breath, she said she was going out for coffee. I told her if she didn't want to get out of the car, she could use the drive-thru. She must have appreciated the advice; Captain Obvious got a kiss before she left.

I set to work on the super suit and quickly decided that a one-piece, white spandex suit made things…well…too obvious. A cape was also out of the question because it was too dangerous. I have a hard enough time with an umbrella in the wind much less a cape. A cape could get caught in a door, burst into flames if too close to a fire, or worst of all, get pulled on constantly by little kids.

Two hours later, The Wife returned to check on my progress. After trying on all the spandex I could find and ruining one pair of The Wife's pantyhose, I had finally given up on the idea of a super suit. Instead, we decided that for Captain Obvious to wear a costume would actually be too obvious. I'm staying incognito by wearing regular clothes and spreading my obvious observations only when I'm away from the house. That way, Captain Obvious can enjoy the life of a superhero – and continue to stay happily married.

Before writing this story, I truly thought chocolate had an expiration date. Even though Best Friend Mitch tried to warn me otherwise, I didn't listen. As always, The Wife showed me the error of my ways. She also informed me that the more expensive the chocolate the better it was for my health – better for my health not to throw it away.

Chocolate Has No Expiration Date

I've tried to save money all my life, and I'm ashamed to say that to date, I've utterly and completely failed. Oh, I've tried! I've clipped coupons that I forget, leave on the kitchen table, and go grocery shopping without. The coupons finally end up in the trashcan long after they expire. I'll go behind The Boy and cut off light switches in an effort to save energy – only to forget and leave the outside flood lights on all night.

There's one thing I won't do in my efforts to be frugal. To me, all food has an expiration date, whether it's stamped on the package or not. When that date is reached around our house, food gets thrown out. This is a hard and fast safety rule I've followed since my college days. It started after I ate that fuzzy green thing in the back of the refrigerator and got really sick – missing classes for a week. Should've known it wasn't gonna be good when it snarled at me. But back in the day, they didn't print expiration dates on things – at least not like they do now. Nowadays you'll be hard pressed to find anything without an expiration date.

For example, milk has an expiration date stamped on it. So does orange juice. Cheese has a "Do not sell after" date printed on each block. Butter, bread, and now even beer have "Best if used by" dates. Even yogurt has an expiration date. I don't know why – isn't yogurt just expensive, spoiled milk? Guess that fuzzy green thing has gotten a bit tastier since college.

The lessons I've learned taught me that everything someone could eat, drink, or use to power a remote control had an expiration date, and sooner or later, these items would no longer be good. But I was wrong. Friend Mitch told me last week that, even though it too has a date stamped on it, one delectable item stays good forever.

How is any of this information gonna save you lots of money? One word: Valentine's Day. Okay, that's two words, but just read on, dear reader, you'll see. This Valentine's Day, I've found a surefire way us men-folk can save a bundle.

Chocolate has no expiration date.

Not being sure, I asked the one person who I knew would know the answer – the expert on chocolate around our house – The Wife. To my surprise, she said that Mitch was right – chocolate doesn't have an expiration date, but husbands do, and if I wanted to know when mine was, just let her find out I threw away any of her stash of expensive, Swiss chocolate stuff.

I'm trying to save every dime I can since out of state tuition for The Boy is really expensive or, depending on your priorities, it's a big pile of chocolate bars. So how will I stay frugal around this chocolate time of the year and still stay happily married? Well, I think I've come up with a way.

This year for Valentine's Day you should do what I'm gonna do. Don't go out and spend a bunch on assorted chocolates in a heart-shaped box. Save your money. Since chocolate never goes bad, just use some leftover chocolate from Halloween or that chocolate bunny from last year's Easter basket. That will show the special someone in your life you care enough to give the best gift of all: the gift of savings.

On second thought, you better not. If you do, your expiration date as a husband could be up earlier than expected.

The Wife is my muse. Her playful outlook on life is contagious and is the source of many of my stories. She is a joy to be with and amazing to watch as she lights up any room she enters. The best advice given to the youth of today is this: marry someone that treats you like an adult but is not afraid to act like a child. Make sure they make you laugh. Laughter will keep both of you young forever.

Ghost in the Woods

The wind carried the odd crunching sound and the laughter of the little girl past my ear once again. And again I turned around – only to find no one standing there but The Wife with an odd look on her face. Had she now heard it too? It had been over an hour, and our walk through the woods surrounding the lake had been uneventful – except for the crunching and the laughter. Both had started soon after we entered the woods.

The deeper into the forest we traveled, the more the pine tree canopy above thickened, screening the harsh afternoon sunlight and defusing it before reaching the moss-covered ground below. The effect cast the forest in a cool constant twilight. Maybe that's the condition most favorable for ghosts to visit. For visit us one did.

The pathway we followed wove through the woods, eventually leading us to a small open field of grass, flattened by deer from evenings past. It was a perfect place for our picnic and a short respite for our ghost. I wouldn't have thought that ghosts need rest, but they must. What else could explain why the laughter and crunching finally ceased just as we entered the clearing?

Afterwards, we continued our walk. Nearing the end of the path, the woods thinned as the lake came back into view. A gentle wind blew, causing diamonds to shimmer and dance on top of the water. We paused to take in the sight. With the pines now behind, the ghost receded back into the woods – waiting for us to revisit her when our busy lives permitted. A hug and a soft kiss on the neck came from behind me. The Wife, she was smiling.

As we drove away, I couldn't help but wonder. Had anyone else walking through the woods surrounding the 100-acre lake ever been visited by the little girl ghost? Once back home, it was back to the stresses of our lives and time to get ready for the coming day of work.

Unbeknownst to me at that moment, my question would be answered later that evening.

I switched off the lights, kissed The Wife goodnight, and settled in for what I thought would be a relaxing night's sleep. Thinking back on the events at the lake and a perfect afternoon spent with the one I love, sleep slowly started to wash over me. All was again right with the world. The ghost, the crunching, and the laughter were finally fading.

Then I heard the laughter once again. Only this time it was much closer, much softer, and even a bit sad. I switched on the lights to ask The Wife if she had heard it too, but she was already asleep – a faint smile tugged at the corners of her mouth. Finally, as sleep reached out and grasped the last conscious thoughts from my mind, I understood. The little ghost from the haunted forest had followed me home and now lay asleep beside me.

We all have ghosts. They're our memories from the past, both good and bad, forever part of us. It's our choice which ones we let visit to enrich our lives, which ones we let pull us down, or which ones we keep hidden away because they're too painful to be revisited by the living. I think only with age can one truly balance them and discern which are which.

For an hour, The Wife took childhood enjoyment out of crunching pine cones on a walk around the lake. And with each crunch, stress left her body to be replaced by the fond memories of a six-year-old girl walking in the woods. We should never forget the joy of being a child. Some ghosts from our past are best kept hidden in plain sight.

Find a positive person. They'll raise you up and make your life wonderful, like The Wife has made mine. In any situation, she can find the positive. I wrote a story for the local newspaper after 9/11. The editor enjoyed it so much he asked me if I could write another story the following week. I went home and asked The Wife what she thought. She said, "If you have something to say, then you should keep writing. When you don't, then you should stop." Twelve years and over 600 stories later, I'm still writing. I'm positive that you should stay away from negative people.

Negative vs. Positive

There are two types of people in the world: those who look at the world and see the positive and those who see the negative. Sure, "in-betweeners" do exist, but only as a singularity in nature. Once joined with a negative or positive, they quickly take on the personality of their long-term partner.

If a positive person marries a positive person, their life is simply wonderful. The sky is bluer, the air is fresher, and even the birds sing louder. Together they can meet any challenge. Their life is full of laughter, joy, and all the things Christmas specials are made of. Positive people stay married to each other because to do otherwise would be negative.

It's a very different story if two negative people marry.

Mr. King was my tenth grade math teacher at Briarwood High – home of the Mighty Buccaneers. The entire year he taught us two negatives made a positive. In math, this may have been right, but in real life if two negative people marry, it's all but a positive thing. Unless, of course, you believe that it will positively be a bad thing if this occurs. In that case, you and Mr. King are correct.

Negative people feed off of each other and, believe it or not, become even more negative. You may know couples like this. No matter how much good happens in their lives, they're still miserable. Their dire predictions soon become self-fulfilling. Think negative thoughts, believe negative things will happen, and sooner or later, they will. When you find yourself around people like this, I have but one suggestion: run away as fast as you can away!

Negativity is like a black hole in space. It'll suck in all who happen to come near – never to be seen or heard from again. Eventually all that negativity wears on a person, and they start to get sick. Don't believe me? Here's a little test. Go to any business, find the person who calls in sick all the time, and you will find the most negative, miserable person employed there.

For the most part, negative people are hard to pull apart. They will stay together in their misery. Unless, of course, one of them meets a super negative – then the attraction is so strong a split will occur. The split sends the lone negative person spinning out of control usually ending them up in jail. Don't believe me, again? Visit any jail. There's not one positive person incarcerated.

Luckily, I've found the rarest person in the world to spend the rest of my life with – a super positive. A super positive literally lights up a room when they walk into it. And people gravitate towards them. You've seen them at parties; they're the ones in the middle of the group of people laughing. So much positive energy comes off them that you actually feel better about yourself just being near – or being married to them.

So what happens when a super positive marries a somewhat negative? She turns that person into a positive. Mr. King, I guess the last twelve years of marriage has proven you were wrong – a super positive and negative equals two positives.

Unfortunately super positives do have one drawback – their energy is soon depleted and needs to be recharged regularly. Hang on, my love; our trip to Asheville will be here soon. You'll have five days to recharge.

The Wife is currently taking quantum statistics for one of her doctoral classes. I wanted her to ask the professor if, on a quantum level, two negatives still make a positive or if they just make a black hole and suck everything good out of each other and all who come in contact with them. She laughed and said, "I'm positive; I'm not going to ask him."

See, I told you. She's a super positive.

This story will finally explain why men are constantly being accused of not listening. And why women have to repeat themselves so many times just to be heard. It's usually because they're talking to men. The reason why men don't listen? Well, for that answer, you'll just have to read the story.

One-Track Mind

This one may just get me banned from the men's club for life, but it's hard to argue with The Wife – especially when she's right. Yesterday, she was talking about how men can only think of one thing at a time. We have a one-track mind. And it seems we men folk are easily distracted. Now, I know this is what we were discussing because, according to her, she had repeated herself three times just to get my attention.

To be honest, I don't really remember how many times she had to repeat herself. During our conversation, a giant lunar moth had landed on the kitchen window screen. In my defense, it's rare for one to see an orange and green lunar moth during the daylight so I was a little distracted.

She also said that men are inclined to forget things – especially dates. Quickly, I defended my gender and reminded her that for twelve years I've never forgotten our anniversary. That's when she reminded me we had only been married for eleven and it was her idea to have the date engraved into our wedding rings. Like I said, it's hard to argue with her when she's right.

Not wanting to lose yet another argument, I also reminded her about how organized I was when we moved into our new home. With my system, we knew where everything in the kitchen was located. At a glance, I could tell her what was behind all the cabinet doors and in each drawer. Never mind that I was helplessly lost when she took down all of the post-it notes; that was beside the point. While they were up, I never forgot where anything was.

She countered with the fact that I can't even find things in the refrigerator – a big rectangular box that has but one way in, one way out, and a huge door. Again in my defense, I said that finding anything in the refrigerator is easy – just as long as I don't have to look behind stuff; having to look behind stuff is simply asking too much of us men folks. That's like actually expecting us to hit the laundry basket, turn socks right-side-out, and not be irritating when you're tired or don't feel good. Don't you think that's asking a little much? After all, we're men. It's in our DNA. But I digress – and no, I didn't get distracted – I simply digressed.

This morning before we went to work, I asked The Wife to sit down at the kitchen table. We needed to have a little talk. I don't know the difference between a little talk and a big talk, but little sounds better. It had taken all night, but I finally had come up with a sound argument that proves once and for all that men don't have a one track mind and aren't easily distracted. And that's the moment when the giant orange and green lunar moth landed back on the window screen. Only this time he brought a big yellow friend.

After finishing her coffee, The Wife got up, kissed me on the cheek, and gave me a hug. "When you remember what you were going to say, call me. It's time to go to work."

You know, for the life of me I still don't remember the brilliant argument I'd come up with last night. It wasn't a bad day though; at least I remembered our lunch date. Lucky for me there was a post-it note stuck on my steering wheel. Strange, I don't remember putting it there.

As a boy growing up in the south with three brothers, I'd thought I had played all the outdoor games possible. The Wife and I took an afternoon walk across a water bridge and quickly I realized there was still one game left to play.

Pooh Sticks!

When the sun slowly disappears below the horizon, a struggle begins in the heavens. Orange and purple hues streak across the sky, fighting against the coming night. There's only an hour left before the battle is lost. Just enough time for a walk with the one you love. It was on one of these walks with The Wife that we came upon an old wooden bridge.

She picked up a stick, walked to the center of the bridge, and did the oddest thing. Dropping the stick over the upstream side, she scampered to the downstream side and leaned over the railing so far I thought she would fall in – potentially lost to me forever. I ran over and tried to pull her back to safety, but there was no need. She wasn't in any real danger.

I watched as she searched the gently flowing water beneath the bridge – for what I did not know. I watched as the lady I loved turned into the seven-year-old pigtailed girl from Virginia I've seen every now and then during our marriage. Revisiting a role she'd played many times before in the heat of midsummer days, her normally quiet voice suddenly filled with excitement, and she shouted, "Pooh sticks!"

She had spied the stick escaping the grasp of the shadows beneath the bridge. A smile slowly spread across my lips, and I watched as she ran, collecting more sticks, only to throw them one at a time over the railing. It was a childhood game – one I didn't understand. After fifteen minutes, the laugher of the little girl finally subsided and reality set back in, but not before exhausting the supply of sticks – and the lady I love. For as much as she may want to be, she's no longer that seven-year-old pigtailed girl from Virginia.

On the slow walk back home, The Wife explained the game. Whenever Winnie the Pooh and Tigger would cross a bridge, they'd take turns tossing sticks over the edge and watch as they disappeared – only to reappear on the downstream side. Then they'd yell, "Pooh Sticks!" With a bridge right down the street from where they lived, The

Wife and her sister played Pooh Sticks every day during the summer. Somehow the game made the oppressive heat of a Virginia summer bearable for a while.

I explained to her that down here in Georgia, we had done things a little differently to escape the heat. My brothers and I hurled dirt clods at little green army men. They were the enemy hunkered down in bunkers dug deep into clay banks under the football stadium where the sun didn't shine and there was always a breeze. At least we thought it was a breeze. The wind could've come from Bubba Hanks. He did eat beans most every day for lunch during the summer.

When we were young, those dirt clod wars lasted for hours. Afterwards, the victors (and that was always us and not the little green army men) would make a trip to the Dairy Queen for a Mister Misty Brain Freeze ice-cream float and then hike down behind Old Mrs. Crabtree's house to dive into the ice blue swimming hole of Cripple Creek.

Years later, when we attended Briarwood High, the wars continued only lasting twenty minutes before each home game of the mighty Buccaneers. I'm proud to say in our five years spent at Briarwood the stadium was never taken, and we big strong football players suffered no casualties. Unfortunately the same could not be said for the opposing side. Many an army man was left on that battlefield.

Be it games of Pooh Sticks or defending an entire football stadium from an army of little green men, playing games are an excellent way of keeping kids' minds off of the oppressive heat of these long summer days.

With sweat pouring off of us, we finally made it back to our home. I told The Wife I would see her in an hour and headed to the coolness of the basement. She called after me as I walked down the steps, "What are you going to do down there for an hour?"

I answered, "I'm going to play my favorite adult summer game. It's called Enjoy the Basement Air-Conditioning."

It really took seven years to get the time to unpack all the boxes in the basement. The passport was placed on the kitchen counter as reminder of the promise we made to travel the world. Two years later, as of this publishing, we will take our first trip to Italy in the spring. If we're lucky, we'll buy a bunch of stuff, box it up, and store it in the basement. And open it in another seven years.

Spring Cleaning

Once again, the all too familiar scourge has descended upon this town, covering everything in a gritty yellow powder. Yep – pollen season is upon us once again, and pardon the pun, it's nothing to sneeze at. Unlike other springs, though, somehow this year we went from winter straight into summer. Lucky for me, I was inside all last weekend cleaning out the basement. Yes, dear reader, it's spring cleaning time.

The Wife and I have been in our house for almost seven years now. I figured it was about to time to unpack the boxes in the basement. Really it was her idea – something about finding Blenko vases. Now, I don't profess to know the difference between a Blenko vase and a Wal-Mart vase, but they were important to her. That's all that matters. And that's why I spent all weekend looking for them.

It's truly amazing what one can find in boxes that haven't seen the light of day for over seven years. My rule of thumb has always been that if you haven't touched it for twelve months, then you really don't need it anymore. It's time to throw it out. When I told The Wife my rule of thumb she replied, "Blenko vases you don't throw out. Husbands with silly rules of thumb are another story."

When I heard her reply, I put my foot down! I'm the man of the house and quickly put my other foot down. I continued putting my feet down . . . eventually reaching the basement and the thirty or so unpacked boxes. You say you don't have a basement? Then just look in the attic or tucked away in the bottom of closets. Odds are you have a bunch of unpacked boxes and maybe a Blenko vase or two.

In the first box, I found my passport. Eight years ago we each had gone through the rigors to procure one. Travel and see the world. Yep, that's what our dream was. Unfortunately the way the economy is now, I don't really need it anymore, but it was still good to find it nonetheless. I put it back into the box and marked the outside "Dreams yet to be fulfilled."

In the next box I found something almost as good as the passport – my original birth certificate. I sure had a small foot back then. I lost it about ten years ago. My birth certificate – not my foot – I still have both of those. I also found the certified copy of my birth certificate provided by that nice person down at the department of vital records after a three-day wait in line. Okay, so it really wasn't three days. It just seemed that long. And if I'm being honest, the nice lady wasn't nice either. I marked the box "Small Beginning."

Around box fifteen was the biggest find of all. In the bottom was my diploma from Briarwood High School, home of the Mighty Buccaneers. Included was a picture of a much younger me, sporting shoulder-length blond hair, throwing a graduation cap in the air with one hand and displaying a peace sign with the other. I marked the outside of the box "Clueless" and gingerly packed both the diploma and picture away. I really miss my hair.

And so it went for the better part of two days. I found many treasures and long ago memories. And in the last box I even found those Blenko vases. Emerging from the basement with arms full of the trademark blue glass, The Wife danced her happy dance. Then she asked me a question. "So are you going to re-think your rule of thumb?"

I answered, "Yes. From now on when I look through boxes, I'll start with the last one first."

A multi-tasker I'm not. I can work all day and never get anything done. Because I'm easily distracted, even writing this article about being distracted took two days.

The Art of Time Management

This morning, The Wife gave me a hug and kiss as she always does before leaving for work. I watched her walk to the car, and then she turned back around, smiled, waved goodbye and said, "If you have the time, could you put away the dishes? Don't get all wrapped up in one of your projects, or they'll still be there when I get back. I love you, but we really need to work on time management."

Of course, I knew by "we," she meant me. I still waved and smiled, then went in to unload the dishwasher. The Wife would be back in about ten hours. Unloading the dishwasher would only take about five minutes – an easy task – even for someone who suffers from chronic ATM disorder.

I've been suffering from adult time management disorder as long as . . . well . . . I've been an adult. Reaching for the dishwasher door, I heard my cell phone ringing somewhere far off in the distance. Before I could get to where it was, it stopped. That started an hour-long search that finally ended only when Best Friend Mitch called again. The cell phone was under a stack of pillows. Why, I don't know. My theory is one of the cats dragged it there.

I opened the door of the dishwasher and started to unload the dishes. Mitch first said he had called earlier and when I didn't answer, he figured I'd lost my cell phone again. Then he complained about all the noise so I had to stop the unloading. He was having a crisis over at his house, and he desperately needed my help. With only having to unload the dishwasher on my "Honey Do List," I did what The Wife would have wanted me to do. I drove over to help my buddy out.

Around lunchtime, the crisis had been averted when my cell phone rang again. It was Robert. I hadn't heard from him in over a year. So when he invited me to lunch and offered to pay, I couldn't turn him down. Besides, I knew that's what The Wife would want me to do. After a lunch of a giant baked potato stuffed with mounds of BBQ, I was also stuffed. Home by 1:30, it was definitely time to put away those dishes – right after a short afternoon nap.

The short afternoon nap ended up being a long afternoon nap that lasted almost two hours. Luckily, I woke up to a gray and black cat licking the last of the BBQ sauce from my face or I'd still have been asleep when The Wife got home. After couple of big stretches by me and the cat, I was out of bed, refreshed once again to take on the rest of the day. If only I could remember what I was supposed to do. With a shrug, I made my way to the kitchen to get a glass of water and wash cat slobber off my face – only to run right into the door of the dishwasher some dummy had left opened.

Curled up on the floor holding my bloody shin, I quickly realized the dummy was me. The gray and black cat head-butted me, paused, and not detecting any additional BBQ sauce, slinked over to the litter box. I hobbled to the bathroom with a roll of paper towels wrapped around the gash in my leg. Now, if I could only find a Band-Aid.

The fruitless search for the box of Band-Aids ended around 5:00. That's when I finally realized that was the item I forgot to pick up at the drug store last week, along with four or five other things I still can't remember. A glance at the clock let me know I could make a quick trip to the grocery store, come back, start dinner and still have time to put up the dishes. That is, if I could just find my car keys.

The Wife got home by six to find the man she has loved for over twelve years on his knees, paper towels wrapped around one leg, trying to fish out car keys from under the refrigerator with a bent metal coat hanger, and a gray and black cat looking curiously on with big yellow eyes, amused that her handiwork had warranted so much attention. I didn't look, but I'm sure she had to be laughing. The cat – not The Wife – The Wife just walked over, opened the door to the dishwasher, and began putting up the dishes. She asked, "So how did your day go, honey?"

"Just fine – you know – the usual." She gave a knowing smile just as I pulled out my keys and sat back on the floor with a sign of victory on my face. The cat walked over and gave me another head butt. The Wife knelt down, bandaged my wound with the Band-Aids she had picked up on the way in, and gave me a kiss. She went into the bedroom, and I put up the last of the dishes, and then joined her. It had been a good day after all.

Yes, there really is a Husband Bench. The Wife and I saw it one day as we walked around exploring the many shops of the downtown area of our new quaint Southern town. We had just moved and, after twelve years of marriage, she finally found the perfect gift. The perfect gift is for a Husband who's irritated about walking through a gazillion little shops. It's a place The Wife can banish him when he gets annoying – The Husband Bench. And knowing me the way I do, I'm certain the Husband Bench will be used quite often. At least it's comfortable.

The Husband Bench

Looks as if someone has finally made the perfect gift a wife can give a husband for Fathers' Day – The Husband Bench. Now as loving and caring an act as it may seem, in reality, an entire bench made just for your loved one is anything but. The husband bench is where the husband is sent when he is being irritating, bad, or otherwise just plain unreasonable. It's kinda like the timeout chair in Old Mrs. Crabtree's third grade class at Mt. Olive Elementary School. At least that's what parents call it today. We kids had many names for that chair, but I can't write about them. This is a family column after all.

For some unknown reason, I spent a lot of time in that chair, and it looks like I'll be a permanent fixture on our new piece of outdoor furniture. It was placed in a corner – Crabtree's timeout chair, not the husband bench. The Wife placed our bench on the front porch so all could see. Utter a cuss word in her class and Crabtree sent you to the timeout chair. Funny – now if I cuss, The Wife banishes me to the husband bench. I wonder if she's talked to Mrs. Crabtree.

Throw just one spitball or don't clean up after yourself and you'd have been planted on the timeout chair for the rest of the day. Luckily, my days of hurling mouth wads of wet paper have long passed, but the "making a mess and not cleaning up" part of my life is alive and well. Since the third grade I've grown considerably, and so has my ability to make a mess. Gazing around our cluttered office as I write this article, I've come to realize something really important. An additional cable outlet would be a good idea on the front porch – right next to the husband bench. Looks like I'll be spending a lot of time out there, and it's soon to be football season.

Now, some of you may think the husband bench is the invention of an idle mind – a stretch for an idea to write about, but I assure you, it's not. The husband bench is real and made by the Amish. On Memorial Day, The Wife and I saw it for sale by a vender set up in our town square. The bench was indeed made by the Amish, but the sign above it could have been placed there by the salesperson's wife. In either case, they thought it would be the perfect gift for our upcoming wedding anniversary. "They" would be The Wife and the salesperson's wife. I didn't think it was a good gift, but seeing as I didn't have a vote, I did what any good husband would do. I helped load the bench on the delivery truck.

I told my dad about The Wife's recent purchase. When he finally stopped laughing, I informed him that, with a quick change of a sign, the husband bench can be made into a dad's bench and shipped to his house in Florida. That's when he reminded me of something I almost forgot. Dads are always right and would never be put in timeout. And being a dad, who am I to argue with such logic? I'm sure if asked my son, The Boy would agree.

You really don't know what you have until you lose it. Dad lost everything one cold winter morning and has never been the same. When two people marry, they become one. How can either continue living just as a half?

Richest Man in the World

After years of hard work, raising four children and seeing them through college, the gentleman still was able to retire at age fifty-two a very wealthy man. Unfortunately, for the man who had everything, it wouldn't be long before his life took a dramatic turn that sent it in a direction he could never have imagined – all due to events not of his making. Life often does that.

A year later, gun smoke gray clouds hung heavily over his head as the late afternoon thunderstorm rumbled closer in the distance. It would be the worst storm he had ever been caught in, one from which there would be no safe haven. Soon golf ball-sized hail would pound him, and cold wind gusts of over fifty mph would tear at his clothes, but for now it was the eerie calm before the storm. All was solemn and still at the gravesite.

A single red rose was placed on the ground. It was always a little joke between them – the gentleman and his wife of thirty-three years. Early on in their marriage, he would often say, "One day, I'll make enough to buy you a dozen roses!" The lady had blessed him with a wonderful life and five children. Yes, just a year earlier, he was a rich man looking forward to retirement and a lifetime spent with his soul mate. Now, as he turned to walk away, he was a poor man. He had forever lost the most valuable thing of all: the only woman he ever truly loved.

The storm hit in all its fury before he reached his vehicle; it pounded his body, but he didn't care. He was already numb. That day had changed the gentleman– he would never be the same again. A large part of him, the best part of him, was left under that rose. Within a month, he moved away. He moved away from his four grown children. He moved away from a lifetime of memories – too painful to remember, too painful to forget.

The gentleman has now lived another thirty years, taking care of their four children, giving advice when asked and money when needed, but most importantly, he has given his love and understanding that only comes with the passage of time. Thirty years – a lifetime for some – but if asked, as those gun smoke storm clouds form behind his eyes and his once strong body slumps against the fierce wind raging in his soul, he will answer that his life really ended that afternoon some thirty years ago.

I make it a point to phone him every day – not just on Father's Day. It's the least I can do. After all, without him, I wouldn't be here. The gentleman has taught me much about life, and I've tried to pass the knowledge on to my son. Still, at fifty-two, I have much to learn.

Tonight I find myself alone again. It has been ten days since The Wife left on her business trip. Tonight, after balancing the checkbook, it feels like we will never survive this economic storm. At fifty-two, the gentleman retired a rich man. At fifty-two, it looks like I will be working another ten years. In the morning, I'll clean the house, finish the laundry, and await The Wife's return. All will be right with the world.

Cutting off the computer, I suddenly feel ashamed. I remember something that gentleman said to his children as he climbed back into the car that stormy day so many years ago. "If you have your health, your children, and the one you love, you are wealthy beyond measure." On this Father's Day, I still have all three. I'm truly the richest man in the world.

When we were married, we became as one. Is it any wonder then when The Wife's gone, it's hard to accomplish even the simplest tasks? How can I do anything when I'm only half a person? If this story makes me seem like a hopeless romantic, then I'm guilty. I love her more now than when we were married so long ago, and I didn't think that would be possible. I don't know how it would ever be possible to live without her. Hopefully, I'll never have to find out.

The Wife's Return

It has been seven days since The Wife left me. I truly didn't think I would survive even this long. The simplest tasks have become incredibly difficult. Like trying to locate where I last placed my shoes. I know I had them on when I came home, but someone must have moved them. I think it must be one of our cats.

It has been 168 hours since The Wife left. Decision making on almost any topic is now impossible. How much do I tip the waitress at lunch? Just what were those stocks we need to invest in? And where did I leave my car keys? Like my shoes, I know I had them when I got home last night. At least I think I did. Maybe the dog has buried them in the woods.

I turn around and ask for advice, but there's no answer. My voice just echoes off the walls. The house is warm when The Wife is present and so very cold in her absence. Our two cats search out warmth in the sunbeams, but other than being really good at sleeping most of the day, they're not much help. Our dog has long since stopped listening to the endless prattle of a lonely man. He's gone outside to find some quiet and is wandering somewhere in the woods. Neither the cats nor the dog know where my shoes are or what stocks I need to invest in.

Twelve years ago next month, in front of a gathering of our closest friends, The Wife and I were made one. Is there any surprise I can't function without her? From the start in our marriage there have been three "B's": beauty, brains and brawn. I have one of the three. The beauty and brains are now gone.

It has been 10,080 minutes since The Wife left. Cooking for two is much harder when there's only one in the house, but the dog has really loved all the leftovers. For some of you, it may be no surprise that The Wife has finally left me. Others may ask why it has taken this long.

Fortunately, her business trip to three states will soon come to an end and she will return tomorrow night. Unfortunately our reunion will be delayed just a little while longer. Others are in need of her husband. I will be at the fire department until the following morning. There are fires to be put out, people to rescue, and lives to be saved.

Some who see us in public have called us Newlyweds. We still find excitement in the simple things of life: holding hands over afternoon coffee, going for walks around the lake at sundown, and stealing upside-down kisses whenever the mood hits us. Welcome back, my love. I'm now made whole.

When you walk in the door, the house will warm once again. I'm sure the cats will leave their sunbeams, pad over to give you welcoming head butts and happy purring sounds. The dog will finally come out of the woods again to celebrate your return. Me? I will see you in the morning, and you can rescue me. After all, seven days without The Wife does make one weak.

Now if you can only help me find where I left my shoes, car keys, and tell me what stocks to invest in, all will be right with the world.

Yes, after the story was written, I did buy a man purse. It truly helped me get organized and put an end to lost car keys. Unfortunately, when I lost the man purse, I had to wait until The Wife got home to get the extra set of keys from her purse. Things worked out for the best in the end. At least with the loss of my man purse, the guys at the fire department stop teasing me.

The Man Purse

The Wife and I were coming back from dinner when it happened. I was asked to go where no man should go. The mere mention of the place strikes fear in the hearts of most men. The very thought of going there has brought the strongest to his knees – many have gone, but few have lived to tell about it.

It's a place that women go many times a day without fear, but I know of no man that has gone and come back unchanged. My difficult journey into this uncharted territory started harmlessly enough with a simple request from The Wife.

While driving she asked, "Honey, will you get me some ChapStick? It's in my purse." Oh, the horror!

Fellow Neanderthals out there, I know what you're thinking. You can't believe I've survived the trip and lived to write about it. For a little while there, it was close – nip and tuck – but I pulled through. I've seen things you shouldn't see, I've been places you need not be, but I survived the ordeal, and so can you. That is, if you follow a few of my simple rules along the way.

First rule when asked to get something out of your wife's or girlfriend's purse is simple: Don't! Just hand them the purse. Doing so takes all pressure of performing off you. Trust me – it's the best way. Besides, chances are you'll not be able to find what they're asking for anyway.

And what makes you think you can find anything in something as complicated as a purse? Half the time, you can't find where you put your car keys. Searching through all those zippers, pockets, and buckles, it's enough to make a grown man cry. Not that that's ever happen to me of course – I've just heard stories.

There's a lot of stuff in one of those little things. And just to confuse us men folk, no two are alike. There're different sizes, with straps or without, round or square, but all have one thing in common. They have so many pockets and hidden compartments you'll spend the better part of your life looking for stuff in one of those things. So if you get the chance, just hand her the purse – you'll be better off.

The second rule is similar to the first: If you can't hand her the purse, then hand it off. Maneuver your way nicely out of the high pressure situation by handing off her purse to another female in the car. They can easily retrieve the item needed in seconds – the same item that would've taken you hours to find – if at all.

The last rule is easy: Men lose everything, women lose nothing. Why? Because they're better organized than we are? Nope. They have a purse; we don't.

I say it's time to put a stop to this inequality. Neanderthals out there, unite! Tired of spending hours every week looking for your car keys? Don't know where that elusive book of stamps ran off to? Then the new Man Purse is for you!

Not to be confused with the fanny pack, the new Man Purse is versatile yet stylish and goes with any ensemble. Going to the gym for a quick workout? Just try our athletic gray MP with Velcro closures. Water resistant and sweat resistant, the athletic gray MP is perfect for the Man-on-the-Go. Ready for a night on the town, dressed only in blue jeans and tee shirt? No problem. The nighttime Man Purse with long shoulder strap is the right one for you.

The nighttime MP comes in three colors: battleship gray, blue jean blue and bulldog red. Yes, you too can easily find all of those everyday important items by just looking in your very own Man Purse.

If you decide not to be a trendsetter – the first on your block with a new Man Purse – then I guess you could do what I do with those important can't-lose items like car keys. I just ask The Wife to put them in her purse. That way, the next time I can't find my keys, she not only will know where they are, but she'll be amused and entertained as I spend hours tearing up the house looking for them.

This was by far the hardest story I've ever written, and it was the one that got the most comments. It will bring a flood of memories to some, and to others, it will give pause. Be thankful for what's really important in life because it can be taken away in a moment.

On the Edge of Forever

She's finally resting quietly now. The starched white hospital sheets, void of any warmth or comfort, slowly rise and fall with each wonderful breath. If she awakens, she will want her blue blankie, the one she's had since high school. Old and tattered, it has seen her through many a crisis. Hopefully it will see her through this one.

Before the surgery, she said, "Don't bother to bring it." Then again she said a lot of things before the surgery – the surgery that was to save her life. I have her blankie with me.

It never ceases to amaze me how one's life can change with a simple knock on the door, a letter in the mail, or a phone call – especially if that phone call is from a specialist. The doctor said what they found was unexpected, and we had some decisions to make. Decisions aren't good when the only answers are bad and not as bad.

Wills, medical directives, and burial arrangements are things we've never thought about. Besides, those are life decisions people much older than we are have to deal with. We're too young, too full of life, with too much to live for. We have years before we have to start thinking about such things. Nothing is going to happen to us. We're both too healthy – or so we thought. My family asked how I was going to deal with all of the uncertainty. I told them I'd deal with it the same way I've dealt with adversity all of my adult life. I'll pray and then I'll write about it. Somehow the writing also seems to make things better, or at least not as bad.

God guided the surgeon's hand, and my love's back with me now – just a few feet away. When she awakes, she will want me to leave. That's just like her – always thinking of others' needs before her own. I'll stay as she has stayed for me many times in the past eleven years of marriage.

Did the sheets stop their movement? No, it's just fatigue finally catching up with me. I spent last night at the fire department responding to emergency calls. Now I have one of my own to respond to. Still, I'll sit my vigil until morning. By then, the doctor's rounds will give me a moment outside to regain my courage. And clear my thoughts. And cry. Cry because of what might have been, and cry for all the others whose surgical outcome isn't as good as ours.

She doesn't need to see how worried her husband really is. For the next two weeks, I have to be strong for the both of us. I won't go back to work until she's recovered.

On the edge of forever without the person you love is a difficult place to be. So many people are in hospitals around our town. Most will come home, but some won't. My thoughts are with them and the families they leave behind. The Wife stirs a little, and I hold her hand. Luckily, this time, she will be coming home with me.

How does one live without their soul mate? I hope neither of us ever has to find the answer to that question. Sleep well, my love, for tomorrow is the start of the rest of our life together. And a long healthy life it will be.

ABOUT THE AUTHOR

As of the date of this publishing, Rick Ryckeley has been a firefighter for over a quarter of a century. He started his career riding the tail boards of engines and clinging for dear life on the side running boards of ladder trucks. A veteran firefighter at the time of 9/11, he was profoundly moved by the event and did something he had never done before. He wrote an article for the local newspaper. It was published on the front page. When he asked his wife Becky, "Now what do I do?" She told him to keep writing if he had something else to say. He has written a weekly column ever since.

During his long career he's been recognized as Firefighter of the Year five times, received the MLK Humanitarian Award, and named Georgia Fire Safety Educator of the Year for his work and dedication to the education of children. This love of life has shown through his career and continues to shine through his stories - stories of his wife and son, everyday observations, and the neighborhood kids he knew growing up at 110 Flamingo Street.

Coming soon

Musings from a Really Cluttered Mind

By Rick Ryckeley

Release date: Spring of 2012

Think back on all the adventures you had growing up, and try not to smile. Remember all the trouble you got into – or almost got into – and try not to laugh. If you've eaten cold watermelon on a hot summer day, been goaded into action by daring friends, or felt the chill in your spine from the flashing lights and shrill siren of an emergency vehicle racing down the road, then this book is for you.

This collection of fifty short stories suitable for the entire family also features three amazing real life stories and what happened after they were written. *Roundabouts:* the story that prompted a news organization from England to request an interview with the author. *Genghis Khan and the Five Second Rule:* cited as factual in a university paper. And *Connecting the Dots:* you'll be amazed as seemly random moments are connected over a period of six months. All leading to a remarkable rescue and the life of a kayaker being changed forever right in the middle of the French Broad River!

The Calling
By Rick Ryckeley

Release date: Fall of 2013
A novel

While fighting his first house fire, Samuel Gable committed a fatal error. For that error, he won firefighter of the year. The shameful secret has haunted him for over two decades. His past catches up to him when Rookie, Jeff Hanson is assigned to his crew. Now, Captain Gables' secret has unleashed the most destructive arsonist the State of Georgia has ever seen. And his men are caught in the crosshairs. Who will ultimately pay for Sam's mistakes? Sam, Jeff, or is it the entire town of Handley, Georgia?

Audio CD version of *Musings from a Cluttered Mind* available from www.RickRyckeley.com

CPSIA information can be obtained at www.ICGtesting.com
Printed in the USA
241656LV00002B/3/P